MAFIA TO MORMON

MY CONVERSION STORY

MARIO FACIONE

CFI
Springville, UT

ISBN: 1-55517-794-8

Published by CFI
an imprint of Cedar Fort Inc.
www.cedarfort.com

Distributed by:

Cover and interior designed by Nicole Williams
Cover design © 2004 by Lyle Mortimer

The events portrayed in this book are true but some names have been changed.
It is not the intent of the author to specifically identify anyone other than the
primary character in this work of non-fiction.

Printed in the United States of America
10 9 8 7 6 5
Printed on acid-free paper

Mafia to Mormon by Mario Facione.

ISPBN: 1-55517-794-8 (pbk.:alk. paper)

Library of Congress Control Number: 2004110363

DEDICATION

To a group of young Primary boys at The Church of Jesus
Christ of Latter-day Saints in Michigan many years ago.
They helped me to realize what it was all about.

FOREWORD

It seems in every culture and time period there are villains to be dealt with—the Philistines at the time of David, the Gadianton robbers in the Book of Mormon, the Nazi's, Communists, and today's terrorists. When I was growing up the bad guys we often read about were the Mafia—the Cosa Nostra, the Mob; organized crime stories glorified in books by Mario Puzo and portrayed on the screen by Marlon Brando and other actors with Italian-sounding names. The Mafia or "Mob" was always located in big cities like New York, Chicago, Las Vegas or Detroit. Names like Jimmy Hoffa and Al Capone were infamous household icons. And we knew these people were bad to the core and always to be feared.

Then one of them from Detroit did an abrupt about face because two young men from Utah gave him a strange book that he felt compelled to read. His name was Mario Facione, and he specialized in the theft and black market liquidation of heavy construction equipment. He didn't know how to read very well, so he learned while struggling through the Book of Mormon. He was touched by the spirit of the book and was baptized in 1981, but when he applied for a recommend to go to the temple his bishop told him he couldn't serve two masters; he had to close the door on the past completely.

"But you don't understand, they'll kill me," Facione responded. "You don't just walk away from the mob."

The bishop said there was no other way, so Mario made a decision—he was ready to die, if necessary, for his newfound faith.

After hiding a cache of incriminating documents in a secret locker at the Detroit airport, Facione negotiated life and freedom with past bosses. In the process, his wife left him and he was bombarded with lawsuits that left him financially destitute. But he trusted the Lord and remained resolute in his newfound religion. Today he works in the Detroit temple. This is his story: *Mafia to Mormon.*

~ Lee Nelson

O N E

They were much calmer this time.

I had driven 100 miles north from the cabin where I'd been hiding out to place the second call.

It had been two weeks since I lugged documents that were my life insurance policy at the moment, to Detroit Metropolitan Airport, stowing them in a locker there for safekeeping; fourteen days since I'd told the only people who never let you out of the business that I wanted *out* of the business.

The reaction was predictable. After all, I'd seen others try to venture out on their own, to get out and try to make it alone. I had watched them fall into traps they never knew were there. *Fools*, I thought at the time . . . *fools who should have known better.*

It's like the guy who started getting a little puffed up, started working deals outside of the operation that had been so good to him in the past. It was amazing because he got so confident and they let him go on with it. They let him go. They knew what he was doing but they gave him lots of rope.

But it didn't last.

It never does.

When it became clear the guy was endangering the whole operation, there was a meeting. Like many before it, this top-secret meeting was held in the shop at my Detroit-area trucking business, where those attending were shielded from curious eyes.

They called me in.

"Hey, Mario," one asked. "What do you think we should do with this guy?"

My thought was to cut his tongue out and let him go.

"No good," came the response. "He could still write."

Having a bit of a soft heart myself, I responded, "I'd like to see the guy still be able to make a living."

But it was too late for him. The word was out on the street that this guy was talking. He had sealed his fate with his words.

Moments passed and the inevitable sank in before the words were uttered . . . Elimination.

That was the mob's way.

The only way.

I got up and walked out. I didn't want to have anything to do with *that*. What I didn't know, some lawyer couldn't make me say.

The next thing I knew, the guy had disappeared. Within a couple of months, maybe not even that long, his family ended up totally destitute, totally broke, didn't have a cent to their names. They were turned loose to the wolves.

Now, years later, somewhere in another secret place, they were meeting to talk about me. I figured they had tore through my office to see what was missing—what documents I had made off with. They knew I was smart enough to do that. They'd grilled my wife, no doubt, demanding to know where I was and what I was doing.

My wife didn't know nothing. I used to take off all the time anyway. She didn't think nothing of it when I told her to go stay at her mother's place. They would try to get information from friends, almost like a police investigation. Except they wouldn't say "Hi, my name is 'so and so' and I'd like to ask you some questions."

Instead, they'd come in and grab you by the throat.

I wasn't stupid. I hadn't made it this far on luck. I had plotted this out like the dozens of scams I'd run over the years. I knew as soon as I said I wanted out I was going to get wasted, and it was going to be instantly.

So I had to be very careful about how I made the decision and how I carried it out. I looked loyal to the last minute. I had a plan set. I knew if I was going to do it, I had to run until they cooled off because Italians are a very hot-headed people. I knew they'd have a meeting and the order would come down.

"Get him. Get rid of him. We'll put somebody in his place and move on."

They could do it very easily. Make it look like an accident, the whole nine yards. So I had to set it up before I called. I had to split. I had my car packed with everything I'd need to get lost for a while. I took everything of value out of my office and stuffed about $300,000 into a pillowcase that I gave to a friend I trusted. The rest of the stuff, documents that could blow their operation wide-open, went into the airport locker. My life insurance policy.

So I made the call. It wasn't as hard as I expected, though the reaction was.

I told them I wanted out. That's all. I didn't want my own deals, wasn't asking for anything but freedom and my life. I told them I'd give them a couple weeks to consider the situation and then we'd deal. They were very, very mad, asking me if I was crazy.

"I'll call back in a few days," I said, remaining calm in the face of the fury. "Think it over."

I jumped into my loaded car and took off into northern Michigan to a secluded cabin I owned that no one knew anything about. Six days I spent there, shooting a gun and pondering the cause of my flight from my lifelong friends and business partners. It wasn't a girl, wasn't a better deal. It was the last thing they, or even *I,* a few years before, would have thought of without a hearty laugh.

Religion.

I had found The Church of Jesus Christ of Latter-day Saints. Or rather, it had found me, a second-tier family member who had cloaked himself in normalcy while running scams that ripped off millions of dollars and changed or ended people's lives in an instant.

Me.

But the Church had found me, and I knew I could go on living a lie no longer. Six days I spent in that cabin praying to this God, who had so recently been introduced to me, who had guided me down a path that had taken me to this moment.

After the six days, I traveled far, to a different public telephone, to place another call. I knew they'd all be together, talking about me and what should happen. I called and, predictably, they told me my butt was grass. I knew the only thing saving me was the information sitting like a ticking time bomb in that airport locker. I was a key. I was a tumbler in the lock and without me and the information I had, it wouldn't open.

I was offering them a deal, I said, the documents for my life. "No deals, no deals!" they angrily insisted, their blood still boiling. They were getting hostile, more profane as the minutes passed, but I was staying cool. I couldn't afford to get mad.

"I'll give you another week," I told them when it was clear this was going nowhere. "Think about what I'm telling you" I said. "I'll call back in a week." The phone went dead.

Seven days later I figured I had to get this over with. I just called them up and said I was coming down and wanted to set up a meeting. By then they'd smartened up. They were cool. Yeah, come on down, they said, no problem. We'll work something out, they promised.

They figured they could get me.

T W O

I was fifteen years old when I decided it was time to make it on my own, leave the comforts of my home in Detroit and prove I didn't need anyone. So I ran away. Just packed up a bag of the bare necessities, climbed out the window and shimmied down a grapevine to the ground.

It wasn't that home life was so bad. It wasn't. I just wanted to see the world I heard everyone talk about. I wanted to see it on my own. So I up and hopped a freight train, headed away from everything I'd ever known.

Two days of rattling and shaking down the tracks to who knew where.

Two days without food as the train barreled across the country.

I finally got off, not because I had reached anywhere in particular, but because I'd been joined about sixty miles outside

Phoenix, Arizona, by a drifter who leapt aboard when the train slowed.

You talk about scared. This guy was mean, but he knew his stuff. He talked about railroad cops who came looking for guys like us, illegal riders stowed away in cars. Just outside Phoenix, the old man said he spotted one and yelled at me to jump. After meeting up with the ground, we talked a bit and he questioned me about where I was from and what I was doing.

"Stick with me," he said.

"No thanks," I replied, too scared to stay a minute longer with the man. I took off on my own.

I walked for a ways before I reached Phoenix though I had no clue that's where I'd ended up. All I knew was it was a lot warmer than Detroit. I was dying for a bite to eat when I saw a guy closing his market. This was in the days before there were steel bars covering shop windows. The lock on the door, I quickly deduced, wouldn't hold back a starving runaway. I busted it in and grabbed up a bunch of food and a big bottle of pop.

In a secluded area nearby, away from curious eyes, I lit a small fire and set a can of beans on the flames to heat. That I got from my dad, that and a lot of other skills that eventually came in handy. I remembered the barbecues at the house, Italian Association members milling around conducting silent deals with looks and nods, and my dad telling mom we didn't need a pot for the beans. He'd just heat them in the can, he insisted. I remembered that kind of stuff all the time, like somehow I knew I could use it someday.

Dad knew all about striking out on his own, taking major risks. He was a soldier in the Italian army fighting a losing battle against the Germans in 1917, when he and a buddy decided they'd had enough.

They planned it out very carefully. They knew the Germans were coming the next morning and would likely overrun them. So early the next morning, out in the field of battle, they hid underneath the bodies of fellow Italians killed in the conflict as the Germans advanced.

Armed with long bayonets, the German soldiers jabbed at all the fallen soldiers as they passed through, making certain each was dead. The blade sliced my dad in the arm, who lay motionless under the corpse, while his friend got jabbed in the leg. Bleeding and in pain, the two laid where they were as the battle raged about them. It seemed endless.

Dad dared to opened his eyes and saw there was no one around. But he raised his head a bit and saw the fighting going on around him. He dropped his head back down, closed his eyes and waited for dark. During the night, the bleeding pair slipped off and made their way to Sicily. They later met up with a guy my dad knew. After sending home for his girlfriend, my dad and her stowed away in the hull of a ship heading for America.

Fearful of being captured as an AWOL, dad stayed on the ship as it docked at Ellis Island and eventually got off at another New York port where he was able to slip off into obscurity.

Short, only about 5-foot 2-inches, Dad packed a lot of power both in words and in action. He made his way to Detroit where he worked at the Ford Motor Company before starting his own cement company. He later rose to prominence within the Italian community, a role that basically set me on my life's course. His girlfriend, whom he made his wife in Italy shortly before boarding the boat, was a good lady. They had eight children, including me, born in 1939.

Dad—he was a tough guy with a soft heart. He was the kind of guy that when he said, "Jump," you better jump three feet instead of two or he'd beat the crap out of you. He was powerful, a good fighter. I once saw him throw 400 pounds six feet. He knew how to fight and he knew how to wrestle. He could throw a punch that could practically knock your head off.

Ma loved us kids a great deal and she wanted us to be independent. But somehow, I don't think running away to Arizona at fifteen years old was what she had in mind. I thought about her a lot those first days eating out of a can in Phoenix.

I missed her and her cooking, but I wasn't about to turn back home, come back like a lost puppy or something.

I hung around the edge of Phoenix for the first couple days, getting my bearings and figuring out the best way to survive. I did okay, just needing food. That was easy enough to get; bust into a store and I was set for a night or two.

For two weeks, my bedroom was a space behind washers and dryers in a twenty-four-hour laundromat. If someone came in and used a dryer, that was great because it'd really warmed me up. Other nights I slept in parked cars that drivers left unlocked. I used a nearby stream to clean up once in a while.

Before long, though, I started needing clothes and I figured I'd actually have to buy the shoes because I couldn't break into some place and sit down and start trying on shoes. I figured I had to make a change.

There was no way I could keep living like that. I guessed I'd better get a job but I didn't know how to go about doing that because I didn't want anyone to know my name. I figured someone from home was looking for me and I wasn't ready to be found.

But I walked into this gas station one day and the owner came out, looked right at me and said, "Where you from, boy?" I looked back at him. He had this scrubby old wrinkly face and he wasn't that old. He was just a tough-looking guy.

I looked at him like I was real tough.

"From Detroit," I said. "What's it to you?"

"Come here," he shot back in a gruff voice of authority. "Does your ma know you're gone from home?"

"No," I answered. "I just took off."

He was a rough-around-the-edges kind of guy but he was concerned about this kid who thought he knew more than he obviously did. But he understood me and we understood each other.

After talking awhile, the old man offered me a job at twenty dollars a week, big money in those days, to wash cars, pump gas and change oil at his place. Home was a compressor room at the shop where he set up a cot and I could hang my clothes and the uniform he gave me for work. I didn't steal anymore. Didn't have to. He knew I was a hustler but he never bothered me, never challenged me. I learned a lot from him and I learned a lot from the streets of Phoenix.

I learned how to survive.

Why this guy bothered with me, a punk from Detroit, I'll never know. He was an up front guy and I trusted him. He was married with two grown kids but they never did nothing to me. He told them to leave me alone.

"Let him do his thing," he said.

My thing, at least on Sundays when the shop was closed, was to wander the streets of Phoenix, learning the ropes of street life from veterans much older than I. I stole a car or two, but mainly I watched and learned.

One day, on a Saturday afternoon about eight months after I arrived there, it was quiet, not too much going on around the station when the old man approached me.

"Come here," he said. "I want to talk to you."

We went over to the area where we washed the cars, where we greased up the autos and stuff.

"I think it's time for you to go back home," he said. "Have you called your mother and let her know where you're at?"

"No, I haven't," I replied.

"You better go home," the man continued. "You're getting smart and you're not going to stay here much longer. I can tell you're getting ants in your pants."

I thought he was trying to get rid of me so I asked what it was I did wrong.

"No, no, no," he replied. "You didn't do nothin' wrong. It's just a matter of time and you'll be gone."

I knew he was right. If I didn't go back soon, I'd never go back. So the next day I called my mom and her voice, filled with relief and joy, held no questions, only the words, "Come home.

Come home."

My father's reaction, not surprisingly, was a little more subdued. After taking the phone from my mother, there was no lecture, no threats of punishment. "Okay, had enough fun?" he queried. "Are you ready to come home and get down to business?"

"Yeah, yeah," I responded, knowing exactly what he meant. "I'm ready to be serious."

So at sixteen years old, having proved myself a survivor on the streets and on my own, I went home to my father.

And my fate.

THREE

Going home meant going back to ma's cooking, the family, the house in Detroit and the Italian Association, where my father was something of an institution. Like other minority organizations before and since, the Italian Association existed at first to give workers from the old country a united voice in seeking workers' rights and representation.

Dad, a master of diplomacy and language packaged in a wedge-shaped powerhouse of a man, rose to the presidency of the group. A lot of union heavy-hitters were part of the association. They elected my dad president because, as long as he was speaking Italian, he could get a point across quite effectively. And *everybody* respected his determination.

My dad was smart enough to know that if he stuck strictly with Italians, he'd starve to death, so he made contacts. I had virtually grown up attending meetings and gatherings with my father, doing as he always counseled, watching, watching and more watching.

Of my dad's three boys, I was the most like him. Johnny was too much of a brain, his face always in a book. Jimmy was too small, kind of flighty. But I was the kind of kid who always observed and asked questions. "Why did this happen . . . who was that?"

Maybe that's why my dad always took me with him when the association met. He had a will to succeed that surpassed the limitations of his education, or maybe the lack of it. He knew what it meant to struggle.

Going to the association meetings, for me, meant escaping the streets near our home where I routinely got in fights with other kids who called us greaseballs and threw rocks at us because we were Italian. It meant being around guys who thought my dad was someone important. By extension, I thought, I was pretty important, too.

"Listen," my dad would tell me as we walked through the crowds, "listen to what's going on and pay attention to the people."

By nine or ten years old, I was no longer just an observer, I was becoming a player. There was another layer to these meetings, I soon realized. There was what was officially going on on the surface, and what was *really* going on in a language only a select few understood.

Shrugs of shoulder, glances of eyes and nods of heads relayed messages. My father often told me to be watching for a signal from one guy or another, saying he might miss it in the crowd. I began to understand what he wanted me to do . . . not always the reasons why, but I was learning my role. I was always asking why this, how come that, why'd you say that. And it was all becoming clearer to me.

I was only thirteen or so when I used some of that wisdom to make money on my own off my friends.

Once we were going on a bike trip to Northland, about

a four-hour bike-hike. We took our BB guns because the big thing to us was to shoot birds and squirrels. We were planning this trip and what food we'd take, how much water to carry and everything. I had the best bike because I used to deliver newspapers so I had a basket on the front.

These guys kept looking over at me while we were planning this trip like I was going to carry all the food and all the stuff. I wasn't saying anything while they were all saying, "I'll bring this and I'll bring that." No one ever said anything about how we were carrying everything.

Finally I spoke. "Okay, guys, I know what you're thinking," I said. "You're thinking you'll all put the food and stuff on Mario's bike and you guys will go sailing off while I'm holding the bag."

I was willing to take on the load, I said, under certain terms. They had to pay for any repairs my bike might need and, most importantly to me, supply my food plus two tubes of BBs.

We sat there and negotiated for hours. The kids were pretty sharp and I ended up having to buy my own BBs. I had to work a little harder on the ride but I didn't spend a cent on food. Plus I blew a tire because I had too much weight in the front basket so they had to pay for a new one.

I had a lot of fun making deals even then. It wasn't so much what I got out of it—it was how much I could get away with. It was what I could get someone else to agree with that actually made me the winner, even though the other guy may not realize he was losing out. I knew the skill came from watching my father.

Dad was smart enough to stay mostly clean when it came to the underworld. He had one toe in and the rest of his foot out. He was running a successful and legitimate cement business at the time, but he was involved enough with the other side just enough to get their help if he needed it.

He used them and if they needed him, he would help them out to an extent. Because of that, as a kid and particularly as my dad's kid, they watched me as I grew. As I got older, I used to look forward to the meetings because these older guys would slip me ten or twenty dollars in exchange for a little errand.

"Hey, Mario," one might call in the middle of the crowded hall. "Go over there and get Gino." And usually when the errand was done, there'd be five dollars or so waiting for me. These guys had money, serious money.

But they needed my father to make some of their scams work. His involvement in some things went very deep, especially with the teamsters who were trying to set up a pension fund.

One guy came up with setting up the pension fund as a source of ill-gotten money for the underworld. My dad knew this guy from the old country and the man with the idea approached him.

For the scam to work, the man said, my dad needed to persuade the membership of the Italian Association that establishing the fund was a good idea. My dad was involved in setting up that fund because there were a lot of Italians in the union then. He was also involved in the crooked end of it once he'd convinced everyone it was the right thing to do. Everybody voted on the pension fund and agreed on it. The union went ahead and started collecting money from the guys and then my dad sort of stepped back and let them handle the money.

My dad would get $5,000 or $10,000, every now and then as a kickback. He was involved and knew what they were doing to make the money. My dad was the persuader, not the enforcer. When those guys told my dad to jump, he would just hop a little, and they respected him for it. He had too much power. He had all the Italians in his hands.

When a good deal was made, my dad always was given extra money. But it wasn't like they came by the house, dropped off the cash and said, "Good job." Instead, it all happened at an association meeting.

They would all be eating dinner together and a guy would come up and stick something in dad's pocket. My dad would never look at it until he got home. When he finally peered into his pocket, he'd find $5,000, $10,000 or $20,000.

He knew that somebody, somewhere along the line did something, and because of his being a key player in this deal, they gave him money. He never said anything. Next time he would see the guy, he would just nod his head and the guy knew he was thanking him.

As I got older, I began making more contacts and the guys began to trust me. My dad would watch me close, telling me, "Go ahead, do it, but don't jump in with both feet." From him, I learned the importance of discretion, of not flaunting your fortune and not bragging about your contacts and successes.

Little did I know that advice would one day save my life.

After Phoenix, I spent about six months hanging around my dad and the association before enlisting in the U.S. Army. That was my dad's idea.

"Get yourself squared away with the government," he advised. To this day, the government doesn't know how much they could have done *without* me.

In the meantime, I faced the questions from the elders of the association when my adventure in Arizona ended. Where had I been, they demanded. What had I done, they insisted on knowing. The heavy-hitters watched me close and one of them pulled no punches.

"What did you do while you were away?" he asked. "Did you give yourself a bad name?"

" No," I responded directly.

"Did you steal?" he continued.

"Yes," was my honest reply.

"Did you get caught?" he grilled.

"No," I answered.

The questioning continued.

Did I kill anyone, he wanted to know . . . did I dishonor the family name, he persisted.

Apparently I gave the right answers because when he was

done, he said, "You go and do what your dad wants. Later on, I want to talk to you."

What he and the others were doing was priming me, though I didn't know it at the time. Dad knew did, though.

"Be careful and smart," he said. "Don't fall in too far."

After I literally bought a GED to get into the U.S. Army, I started what would become a lucrative two-year career in the military. I was assigned first to Fort Carson in Colorado and then to Fort Benning, Georgia, with the 101st airborne division.

An early injury won me an assignment to the motor pool where the higher-ups figured my automotive background would come in handy.

They did me a big favor.

F O U R

I could sniff out a chance to run a scam about as quickly as I could smell the first scent of mama's cooking wafting out of the kitchen. It didn't take too much time in the military motor pool before I realized there was the potential to make a bundle on the black market selling tools, parts and other military equipment the higher-ups never would know was missing.

When I realized how sloppy the inventory and record keeping was, a light went on in my head. But I didn't rush into anything. First, I ran a few tests.

I'd take twenty boxes containing tools like pliers, for example, and move them to a different corner of the warehouse; not stealing them, yet, just changing their location to see if anyone noticed. Time passed and no one said a word. Before long, I was taking fifty boxes at a crack and hiding them in the woods nearby. I moved up from pliers to bigger ticket items.

I began a side business on the black market selling everything from five-gallon gas tanks to full radio systems.

It was so unreal. I couldn't believe it myself. I was working this scam and getting away with it.

Once I took a whole radio system from a Jeep. I got more daring as I went along. These radios were lying all over the place. Like before, I tested the system. I took one radio and put it in the back of the Jeep where everyone could see it, and left. I went about my duties in the motor pool. No one touched it. Next, I took the radio and hid it beneath a panel in the barracks, covering it in gravel and dirt. It sat there for thirty days and nothing happened. Nobody asked me anything.

I used to go in and out of the warehouses like I owned them. In the end, I stole enough radio equipment to set up my whole trucking company when I got back to Detroit.

Business got so good that I had to hire help to transport the stolen items to my makeshift warehouse in the woods. I hooked up with a guy who needed money. But he tipped his elbow too much, throwing back the drinks. I used him for his strong back but I stopped telling him anything because he drank too much. He would spill his guts. I'd give him his booze money and he'd keep his mouth quiet, ask no questions.

He'd take these cans, or whatever the item was at the time, and take them into the woods. There I had another guy who would take them out onto the streets of Boston and sell them. Gas cans turned into tires—turned into ammunition.

The military carefully tracked its weapons back then, but not the ammunition, and it was easy to get my hands on. It would come in boxes, big wooden boxes full of thirty-caliber rounds used in M-1's. I'd get some cases of ammo and take it out into Boston.

Later, when it was known on the streets that I was selling, I had one guy who became a middleman setting up a distribution center of sorts. He then sold the stuff for me while I raked in the money. I sold about 2,500 of the gas cans alone, at ten dollars a pop.

There turned out to be a huge market for the radios and I was selling those for $150 on the street, aside from the ones I kept for myself for later use. I never bothered to add it up, but I figure I made a couple hundred thousand moonlighting on the black market in the military.

When the end of the month rolled around and the other guys were strapped for cash, they'd come to me for a loan. They'd go out and have a wing-ding of a time, they'd gamble and then they'd come back broke. I was the guy with the cash but I never flashed it around myself. Not my style.

I never, never walked around flashing $100 bills. That was about the dumbest thing you could do. And I would never go out and run the town and flock with all the guys at the whorehouses or the bars. I never called attention to myself.

I learned early that if you don't want to go to school for a career, which I didn't, then this was the life. And there were rules. You better not drink, you better not be a big shot and you better always stay low, always be underground because if you get caught being a big shot, everyone is going to laugh at you. And the money you got will all go to lawyers and you're going to end up with nothing. If you're going to play the game, you've got to play it smart.

I made a lot of money in the military but it was piecemeal. It wasn't like I could pull a truck up and take whatever I wanted. It was take two radios here, four tires there, ten to twenty cartons of tools there. It added up. It was all just small, where it wasn't noticed.

And that's how I operated.

I saw an opportunity and I exploited it.

But I never forgot the lessons from my father. The secret to doing things is not getting caught. And the way to not get caught was to do just what my father told me—know your people, how far you can push them, how to use them and never let them have control of what you're doing; and *never* let anyone fully know what you're up to.

I sent my dad $10,000 once while I was in the military. He didn't write English and I didn't want to talk to him on the phone because he taught me never to talk business on the telephone. So I came home on leave once and he took me off to the side to talk.

"What are you doing" he questioned.

Without hesitation, I told him "I'm stealing stuff from the government."

He paused a moment and responded. "Boy, you get caught, you know, and you go to prison and that's it," he said. "There's nothing I can do for you over there," he warned. "Over here, I could help you but over there I can't."

I promised to be more careful and went back to the military, back to the job.

In my family, you never bad-mouthed a woman. If I ever showed a woman any disrespect, called her a dumb broad or something, my dad would cuff me like there was no tomorrow.

"I don't care if that woman's a hooker," he'd say, "she's a lady. You don't ever, ever talk bad about a woman. No matter what she does, you show respect."

You also showed respect to the elderly.

And being a rapist would defame the family name . . . no question. Defaming the family name is a big deal in an Italian family, at least it was in mine.

But there was respect for stealing and not getting caught. The only dishonor would be in getting caught, in failing to get away with it undetected.

I knew messing with the federal government was taking a huge risk, but the temptation was too great. The record keeping was so bad . . . so bad, it was an opportunity staring me right in the face . . . and I couldn't look away.

I hadn't been raised to look away.

It wasn't the money as much as the challenge; you set your

sights. You look at something and you want it to work. If you want it bad enough and you make it work, the money flows.

The key was to keep that money hidden, to not flash it around. I never went out and ran the town or flocked with the guys at the bars. The wrong people might start wondering how an Army guy had so much money to spare. I just never called attention to myself. I knew I'd only get caught if I got greedy or decided to show too much cash around and I wasn't about to do either.

Nobody knew what I was doing except my dad. He never told anyone, though his response when he was asked by the family how I was doing, clued them in that I was hustling.

"So what's your son up to in the military?" they'd ask.

His reply was simple but telling.

"He's making a lot of money."

F I V E

The U.S. Army, unaware of how much it'd lost during my enlistment, gave me an honorable discharge. I went home to Detroit with $60,000 in cash in my pocket from stealing and selling all the equipment over my two-year stint. I also had the radio systems that I stashed at home. They'd come in handy later.

I arrived back home and went to work at my dad's cement business. I never liked the cement business . . . I didn't like the smell of it, but my allegiance to and respect for my father kept me in it.

One night over dinner he made an announcement to my brothers and me.

"I want to retire," he said. "Not totally, but I want you boys to take over everything and I'll help you out a little bit here and there."

My stomach sank, my appetite vanished.

I don't want to do this for the rest of my life, I thought, but I didn't say anything. I didn't want to hurt my father's feelings.

So I kept working at the business, going out on jobs, pouring cement and hating getting up for work each day. I knew I had to get out but didn't know how to tell my father. It really troubled me; I felt like I was letting him down because I hated what he'd done his whole life.

One Friday I went and picked up a new truck I'd purchased and pulled up in front of the house. As was his custom, dad was sitting out on the porch, puffing on a cigar as he watched the neighbors. That was his Friday night ritual. I drove up in this big new shiny truck and said "Hey, pops, how do you like this truck?"

"Oh," he answered. "You boys are buying us a new truck?"

"Well, pop. I bought it," I replied.

"Oh, that's okay," he said. "What are you going to use it for in the cement business?"

"Well, I can haul the broken cement and when the guys do repair work, I can bring sand to the job."

"That's a nice idea," he said, still puffing away on his cigar. Then a moment passed before I spoke again.

"And, too, I can haul stuff for other people," I said referring to a big contractor in town my dad knew. "You know, I can haul some stuff for him."

Boy, he just stopped right there, looked me straight in the eyes.

"You mean you're not going to work with the boys, doing the cement business?" he asked.

He knew right away.

I was still living at home at the time. My folks were getting older and I wanted to watch out for them. Now my dad was watching me closely, as I answered weakly, "When they need me, I'll still help out."

The cigar went in a tray as dad stood.

"You stay here. I've got to do something."

He marched in the house and locked the front door behind him. The next thing I knew he appeared at my second-story bedroom window with a load of my belongings in his hands. Seconds later, they were on the ground in front of me. He continued gathering and tossing until everything I owned was on the front lawn. I could hear him screaming up there. I knew better than to try and go upstairs and smooth things over. He came back down the stairs, onto the porch and, as I snatched up my stuff, said, "Don't ever come back."

I guess you could say he didn't take my decision to leave the family business too well. But about a year later, it all smoothed over. By then my older brother had also left the business and dad had resigned himself to the fact that his boys were striking out on their own.

In my case, I eventually bought a couple of trucks, installed the stolen radios and became a subcontractor on construction jobs, hauling waste away from sites while raking in the money. Some of it was legitimate, of course, but most came from double-dipping on various jobs

I was involved pretty heavy in one of these jobs. I had five trucks down at a site in Detroit and each one of the trucks would haul three loads a day legally. But in a deal worked with the contractor and myself, we'd report they each hauled seven loads.

"You run the trucks," the contractor said. "Pad it and let me know how many you pad."

At the end of the workday, the foreman would sign off on the load tickets, and I made sure to come in when he was extremely busy.

The first night I added one load; the contractor said, "Tomorrow, add two." It was $1,400 a load at the time, so the money was big. When the contractor would get the check in at the site, we'd split the difference. That's why I won the job. No one knew about it but him and me.

Discretion was key. That's what the guys loved about me. I kept my mouth shut. At the end of the month, the checks would arrive and the contractor would say "Hey, Mario, come here," and I'd head into his office. He'd lock the door and he'd go "$1,000, $2,000 . . . that's your cut."

We stretched it over the life of the project. It was a huge project, a major project and we took in $750,000, splitting it between the two of us. That's how I ended up buying more trucks and constructing a building for my business.

None of what I owned was in my name. In those days, if you paid cash no one asked any questions. I bought everything with phony identification so no one had a name to connect me with the properties I eventually acquired.

I bought the land for my business for $75,000 cash and used a fictitious name. I asked the guy how much he wanted and he said $80,000. I said "How about $70,000 cash?" He countered with $75,000 cash and I said, "You've got a deal."

The next day I went over and gave him the cash and he didn't say nothing. I didn't say nothing either. He signed it over to me. We did all the registering and it was done. I was Joe Willy that owned 22 acres of land in Wixom. I eventually had three houses and a trucking company building where I had $300,000 in cash stashed in a pipe.

The scams continued. A lot of what I did, where I made big money, was in heavy equipment. Back in those days when they made heavy equipment it was not registered like an automobile is registered, or a truck is registered. It was put on the street without any way of tracing where it went. In my mind, it was a gold mine waiting to be discovered.

It all started when a friend of mine was doing paperwork for one of the big machine-makers here in the states; he knew there was no way in the world they could trace the equipment once it went out the door.

I didn't have the financing at the time to go out and set up the network I needed to pull off the scam, so I went to certain people, showed them the potential, and *they* set me up.

That was a little gift for them guys. A million here, a million there . . . it was a real kicker for them.

There was the opportunity again, and I knew how to exploit it. A legitimate person might have gone to the manufacturer, pointed out the flaws and then demanded a lot of money to help them close the loopholes.

Not me. I turned it around and took advantage of it, made millions off of it, and became a major player in the end.

When I took the plan to the association boys, they knew it was a good one and if it didn't work, well, it wasn't critical. I would pay the money back and a lesson would've been learned.

It wouldn't have been the first time. There were a lot, and I mean *a lot* of things that we tried, that didn't make money. It wasn't a lot of money but we did lose some. That was not the case this time around, however.

I was always the guy who set everything up. My main function was to make sure it was all in place. There were a lot of things involved—license plate changes, rental of equipment to move stolen machinery, a lot of details that made or broke the scam. Some of these guys who helped out, I ran across once and never saw again. Some of them never saw me. I just talked to them on the phone in conversations the average person would take as legitimate business.

Sometimes it involved people on the inside. If we were bold enough and you had a fine piece of equipment on the job, we would steal it near the end of the job. First I'd contact guys I knew in Ohio telling them I had a backhoe worth $300,000. I'd offer it to them for $200,000 but tell them they had to pick it up the next day. They'd agree and tell me to bring it down and the deal was in the works.

I'd prepare the phony paperwork and go steal the backhoe using the key supplied by the worker who was in on the scam. I'd load it up and take it right down to Ohio where I'd get $200,000 in cash before heading back to Michigan. The construction company would get insurance money on the stolen backhoe and there was no way to trace it.

The business, so to speak, took off and soon spread outside of Michigan, to the east where several deals went down in New York among other places.

I was the one . . . everything went through me.

The biggest score I made was $500,000 in one week. I had eleven guys with trucks that could move equipment and hit eleven different jobs in seven days. For the most part, I remained in the background overseeing the operation. Sometimes, though, I tagged along on the jobs I thought were going to be the slickest, just to get in on the excitement of it.

The money didn't mean anything; it was the challenge and accomplishment. There was no competition. Who thought of it? Who put the whole thing together? Me. But I couldn't do it without having a whole network throughout the country and having the proper people in place to make it work. Gambling, prostitution, drugs, all that stuff was already controlled. But heavy equipment, that was all new.

When I sat down with my partners and said—"Look, here's what you can do. Here's the kind of money to be made, and here's what we have to do to make it"—they knew it was fertile territory.

They were right.

S I X

Success opens doors. The more money I made, the more obvious it became that heavy equipment was producing beyond anyone's expectations, *and* was earning me the chance to diversify.

To the world, I was a blue-collar guy running a trucking company. I was real low-key; that's what they liked about me. I wasn't Mr. Flashy Joe. I wasn't chasing after women, wearing gold chains, giving any hint of the money I really had.

My dad always said, "You'll make a good living if you stay low-key and keep your mouth shut. You better learn how to do that because if you don't, you're going to end up in jail and you'll never end up being worth nothin."

That was the whole thing to me, not being flashy. I ran around in jeans and work boots and drove a pickup truck. I never had a problem with that because I could get away when I wanted to. I'd just make a call and say "Hey, I want to get away for two or three weeks, maybe to Vegas." At the appointed time, there'd be a plane waiting for me at some airport away from Detroit, and it was always first class.

Over in Vegas, I'd play the shooter, drop fifteen or twenty thousand, no problem. Then it was back to Detroit, the jeans and pickup . . . back to work.

Never was I sloppy and never was I overconfident. I ran scared every day. That was part of the thrill. It was a game. And it was a fun game. I was doing something I knew was very sneaky and getting away with it.

It's like going to the store, stealing a piece of candy and not getting caught. Maybe tomorrow you'll go back and try and get two. I loved that. I never drank and was always aware of what was going on around me all the time. The less people around me knew, the less likely I was to get caught . . . and I never did.

I was the only sibling in my family to get involved in the business. My older brother was too much of a hothead. He didn't have the patience. He was spontaneous, a "you-punch-me-and-I'll-knock-you-out" kind of a guy. He even scared my dad because he was so reactionary.

Whenever my dad and I wanted to talk plain, pop would always give my brother fifty bucks and say, "Here's some money. I need to you go to the store and pick this up." Then we'd talk in confidence.

My dad was the only one who knew what I was up to. My mother had an inkling, just a little one. But mothers know what they don't want to know. My dad used to tell her to keep her mouth shut, and she did.

She didn't know half of what my dad was involved in either, and she didn't need to know. She lived her life in blissful ignorance for the most part.

My discretion and low profile made me a favorite with some of the elders in the Italian association. They filtered so much through me and my businesses, it was unreal. That's where the trust was built, and that's when things really started snowballing.

My trucking business remained lucrative, relying largely on the greed of inspectors and contractors who were willing to look the other way to make a buck or two.

I was involved in many other things besides the trucking and the heavy equipment. There was always a good scam going down somewhere, and chances were that I either set it up or helped make it work.

It was the challenge, the thrill of not getting caught that kept me moving from one deal to the next. It was also the memory of a lesson learned early in life that kept me well-respected in my circle . . . never lose your head, don't start imagining you can go off on your own.

That instruction had been pounded into my brain since I was a kid and if that hadn't worked, watching other fools try it and pay a heavy price, did. If there was a deal where you took the money and started playing on the side, well, that's when they started cutting legs off and really hurting you.

There were some times when I felt a pang of what I guess must have been a hint of conscience, but it never really lasted.

One time, some boys and I got the goods on a millionaire I was doing a job for. He'd been foolish enough to tell me he had more than $100,000 in cash stashed in his home. This guy ended up being worth $600,000 to us in the end. We set a scam where he paid us without even realizing what was happening.

By the time he knew he'd been had, it was too late. The way we set it up, we had that old man so excited it was unreal. He was envisioning making millions of dollars in the deal with us. We got him to give us money for something that was non-existent.

When he figured something was up, we went through the house with a couple of guys and found $170,000 in cash that we took. If he ever breathed a word of what had happened, we warned, he'd be stuffed in a sewer.

We walked out of that house and I remember thinking to myself, "Man, I really didn't want to . . . but the money was so nice."

Where are you going to make $30,000 in one day, I asked myself. The old guy never, never said a thing. Every now and then we'd take a ride by his house and he'd be out there cutting his lawn and we'd say, "Hi, how are you?"

Just because we could . . . just to send a message.

It didn't really bother me because I knew neither he nor anyone else I'd scammed could prove anything. They could come up to me and say; "You swindled me out of $600,000." I could look the person square in the face and deny it. Then it was up to them to prove it, and they never could. The way we had it set up, there was no way in the world to prove it, no paperwork to trace.

They could accuse me of a lot of things but they couldn't make them stick.

I found myself getting more and more involved. Because I was low-key and shrewd, I got brought in on things, jobs where the stakes were high but the payoffs were big.

That's when the trust was built and that's when things really took off.

S E V E N

By 1968, I was a key player in about six operations. This was besides the trucking business that provided the front of legitimacy I needed to do the deals that made the real money.

And there *was* real money to be made. The riots in Detroit paid off big for my operation in 1968-69, as reconstruction took place. Equipment was needed. It was a heady time for me and my guys. A lot of the deals I got involved in when they were small, grew and grew. I used a lot of phony names and phony identification to set up or pull off scams. We made a lot of money off the riot and it kept right on going—building and snowballing as my network grew.

It was also in 1968 that I happened to stop by a store and meet my future wife. We talked for a while, I don't recall about what exactly, but it must have been interesting because I asked for and got her number. I called her a couple of weeks later and we started going out.

I didn't worry about the kinds of things a normal guy might worry about in picking a wife. Cooking, for example; I didn't care about that because I already had someone who was doing the cooking. Ninety percent of the time I ate out anyway. Besides, if I wanted good Italian food, mom was still at the stove, going strong.

Lynette, that was her name, had a tight mouth. She didn't tell anybody nothing they weren't supposed to know. I just needed someone for a companion and she was helpful in certain ways, helping me watch my back. When you have a suspicious mind, everyone is suspicious. I couldn't be too careful and she provided me with an extra set of eyes.

She wasn't too interested in money or knowing exactly what I did to get it, but she'd help me out if I needed it. I'd tell her to watch one guy in a certain situation and let me know what he did, how he acted. She didn't ask questions, just did what I asked.

So we got married and it was a mutually beneficial arrangement in most ways. I was doing well and eventually we owned three homes all on the same street. Ours was a ranch-style home adjacent to more than one acre of woods. That suited us fine. Next to it was another home I owned that I rented to a guy I knew, and his family.

The third house, across the street, I also rented out but to more temporary residents. It became a safe house, of sorts, for guys who needed to disappear for a while or hold meetings they didn't need nobody else knowing about.

They would pick up the garage door opener at my office and then slide right into the garage, closing the door behind them. No one could see who stepped out of the car or what they were doing. That was the idea. They could walk right through to the house. Guys who were in trouble, who didn't want to be found used the place quite a bit. Maybe the feds wanted them for fraud or, in a couple of cases, murder. It usually was occupied and I was well paid for its use.

There was cash stashed in the pipe at work, cash I had at home, money from the businesses and payments for deals I pulled. Even though Lynette and I led a somewhat subdued life, we still had to account for having more money than my trucking business alone was pulling in.

So on the advice of our accountant, we set Lynette up with her own business, a cleaning service with a specific clientele. She and her crew cleaned the homes of guys I knew, fellows who would not want strangers in their homes. With Lynette and her girls, they knew their secrets were safe.

I set her up in the business and the guys paid cash. No records were kept, no client lists filed. Don't ask them any questions, I told her and her crew, and if they ask you questions, tell them nothing. Just do your job and get out.

We wanted to show she was working. If we had that business, we could account for some of the income we obviously had. That way if anybody came and started asking where we were getting our money from, we could point to her business as well as mine.

It all was part of the plan, the larger picture. We could account for some money while making some more. My buddies got a service they needed without the questions they feared, and I continued to be a vital link in an organization that seemed unstoppable.

E I G H T

I'd rarely been west of the Mississippi since my youthful stint in Phoenix when, in the spring of 1980, I boarded a plane bound for Salt Lake City, Utah. The destination hardly mattered, of course, it was just another opportunity waiting that drew me to a place I'd barely heard of. I had put money up front to get involved in a deal and was heading out to the place where it would all go down.

I was mildly interested to see this new place, but I figured it would be a little po-dunk town like something I'd seen in the westerns. I figured it would be a gas station, a couple of stores, dirt roads and all that good stuff. The only paved road would be through the middle of town.

Of course, I'd seen towns like LA on the news, spent those months in Phoenix and all that, but I'd never really paid attention to "out west." Everything I did was east of the Mississippi so, except for trips to Vegas once in a while, the west held little interest for me.

My thoughts about the details of the deal I was planning to finalize were interrupted by the pilot's voice through the cabin announcing we were approaching the Salt Lake City airport. Our plane banked and I looked over and saw the rising spires of the granite Mormon temple in downtown Salt Lake. It was the first building I saw. I couldn't believe it . . . all the buildings that were there, the whole scene was quite different from any image I'd had in my mind.

But my eyes were just fixed on the gleaming spires of that temple. I just couldn't believe such a unique, beautiful building was there and all these other buildings surrounding it.

It was just like it stood out with a neon sign on it. I craned my neck to keep it in my view as the plane continued to make its descent. It just stuck in my mind.

The friendliness of the people and the cleanliness of their city struck me moments after I stepped off the plane. It just blew me away. I couldn't believe there was a metropolis so neat, and where people were overly kind.

You'd ask a question and right away you'd get a response. At home, at Detroit Metropolitan Airport, you ask somebody a question and they might answer as they're walking 900 mph away from you. Very seldom do you get someone who will stop and actually help you, direct you, or guide you. Home was nothing like I was experiencing at the Salt Lake airport. It was just unreal to me.

I was met, as arranged in advance, by a young man who was to drive me to Provo where I would meet up with my contacts. As we made our way south through the Salt Lake Valley, I continued to be impressed by what I saw. Everything was so organized. I could just see there wasn't the disarray there like there was at home in Detroit, which, in the '80s, was a mess.

After the riots, city officials never did much. Homes were burned down, the charred shells lining the streets; junk cars were parked here and there. I looked out the car window as we drove and didn't see any of that. I was looking for it but it just wasn't there. I was really, really impressed.

I vaguely remembered hearing about this religion that was supposed to be based in Salt Lake City and asked the kid who was driving me about it. Turns out he was a member of The Church of Jesus Christ of Latter-day Saints, but didn't attend anymore.

He explained a little about the Mormons to me and what they were like. I started thinking about the Quakers, living a funny kind of life, not being in the mainstream of the world. The young man didn't tell me too much more, just that Mormons were very unique individuals. He wasn't bitter, he just said he couldn't be involved with the Church anymore. But he did say it was good, and that the community was good.

He didn't bad-mouth the Church at all, even though he'd decided it wasn't for him. He seemed like a nice enough kid, only about twenty or twenty-one years old, and he worked for the guy I was doing the deal with.

It wasn't long before we entered Utah Valley and made our way to Provo, where I met up with the guys I was doing the deal with. We talked through the specifics, made plans and, at the end of a long day, separated for the night.

I'd just settled into bed in my hotel room and must have drifted off because I soon found myself watching what seemed to be a play. I was the sole audience member and the actors, whoever they were, were talking directly to me. As I sat in confusion, the words came at me. "You've got to do this," one would say before another guy would come at me saying, "You've got to take this road."

It was like they were directing everything at me and I was just stuck in this mass of confusion going, "Whoa. What am I going to do?" I was the only one there, so they had to be talking to me. *Should I take this road they kept talking about?*

I wondered.

The words kept coming, pounding in my mind and I stood stagnant, unable to know what to do. It was like the yellow brick road was in front of me, these guys were all telling me I should follow it, but I couldn't move.

I woke with a start, clearly remembering every detail of what I realized was a dream. I still was filled with confusion about what I had experienced; after all, it was the first time I'd had any kind of a dream like this.

It wasn't that I didn't usually dream. I did. Usually it was about getting caught in a scam or saying the wrong thing to the wrong person. But never anything like this, a dream that seemed to be sending a message; a dream that left me drained and confused, uncertain what any of it meant.

But what did seem clear were the constant references to changing directions, to taking a different road, although I had no idea where that road might take me or even if I wanted to go. I had nothing to relate the dream to, no religious beliefs to tie it to, to refer to for translation.

Whatever its purpose or its origin, the dream stuck with me. The next day I began having a lot of serious doubts about the guy I was working with and the deal we had worked out. I confronted him and told him I wanted my money back. He gave it back and I headed home to Detroit.

The details of the dream still vivid in my mind, I boarded a plane and left Salt Lake City—the clean, organized streets and friendly, helpful residents. Back to the shop, back to the deals, back to a way of life that seemed destined to continue.

N I N E

I'd been back in Michigan exactly two weeks when I returned home one day after work to a message from my wife that sent my blood pressure through the roof.

Turned out that earlier in the day, she'd heard a knock on the door and found two clean-cut young men in suits standing outside. On a normal day, for some reason, she wasn't at work and spoke to the two guys who introduced themselves as Elder Staples and Elder Gardner. They said they were from this church in Salt Lake City. She smiled because she knew I'd just been there on a business trip and told them so.

They handed her some pamphlets about their church and asked if they could come back when I got home. For some reason that I don't think *she* even knew, Lynette said yes. That was bad enough, inviting two strangers who looked a little too clean-cut, back into our home, but it got worse.

At that time, we had a phone line operating in the home that no one knew about but us and two others, including a fellow with the phone company who set it up for me to do my business. It was for calls that I didn't want no one to know I was getting, and the callers didn't want anyone to know they were making.

It was one of three lines in the house, two of which were normal. For some reason when those guys came to the house, Lynette gave them the number to the third line for the call back. She said they could return to talk with me when I was home, but would have to call first. So they left, carrying with them a phone number they should never have had.

When I got home and she told me about giving them that number I was not far from nailing her between the eyes. My mind was flooded with thoughts of all the problems this could cause me, that number being given out. Not only would I be in serious trouble with the people who set the thing up for me, but it would have had a domino effect.

Once the wrong people found out about the line, I'd end up on a witness stand somewhere with a prosecutor demanding to know, "What were you doing with that line?"

It would not have meant the end of the whole operation, but it would have been a serious hit, knocking out about sixty percent of my deals.

So when I knew there were two guys out there with this phone number I got every excited, very mad. I went ballistic and then frantically focused on what I could do, if it wasn't too late, to get that number back and find out exactly who Lynette had given it to. Sure, they'd said they were from some church but anyone, including the feds, could use that line.

I waited for the phone call from one of them. I was really going to jump on the guy, tell him to get rid of the number and all that, really lean on him to never want to have anything to do with that number or me again. My wife told me they were young boys and I figured I could scare them into not doing anything they shouldn't.

But when the call came, it didn't quite go down that way. Instead, as this boy who called himself a missionary for The Church of Jesus Christ of Latter-day Saints started talking to me, something came over me that made me relax.

Before he called, I wanted to meet him and his buddy to check them out, to see if they were what they claimed to be, mainly because I was so panicked about the number being used. But as I talked to the missionary on the phone, I became very calm. And this guy, who I figured I could intimidate, talked with a lot of self-assurance. He mentioned that Lynette had told him I'd been in Salt Lake City recently, so we started talking.

During the long nervous wait for the call, I'd looked at some of the pamphlets they'd left behind, trying to find out what these two were all about. My main concern was to get that number, but when they called I said, "I've never heard of you guys. Do you believe in God?" He said they did.

Next, I wondered why they were going door-to-door. He talked about preaching the gospel and all kinds of other stuff. Finding myself getting interested in this guy's church and less concerned about the phone number at the moment, I kept throwing questions at him about the Mormons and what they believed. I figured I'd stump him with a question about what it was all about.

"Can you give me an answer about why we're here on this earth," I asked.

"Oh, sure," he said, suggesting that we get together to talk about it in detail.

I starting thinking to myself that maybe it'd be good to get to know these guys for two reasons—so I could get some insight into whether they were trying to scam me and also, to try and get them to forget all about the phone number they had. I just felt at ease on the phone because this kid talked with such confidence.

We made an appointment for the next week. But before we hung up, I told him to never call back at that number, to rip it up and forget it. I gave him a regular number and he said that would be no problem. I could tell he was confused by how adamant I was about throwing out the first number, I could hear it in his voice.

Still uncertain about the situation, I went to the guy who had set the system up and told him there'd been an accident, that the number had gotten out to some church organization. I told him to watch the line and see how many calls came in.

I didn't trust anyone. I didn't know if Lynette's giving out the number had been as innocent as she claimed. Maybe there was something fishy going on and maybe she was part of it. I didn't know and my gut instincts kicked in. I just started covering my back, checking everything out.

I wanted everything checked on that line, but the days came and went and there were no calls on the line that weren't expected. This was my way of checking to see if this guy was going to hold up to his word about getting rid of the number, never using it again, and he didn't.

The night of the appointment rolled around and at 6:30 P.M. the two missionaries arrived on time. I had been thinking about them earlier in the day for some reason, wondering what they were going to say. Questions that I'd had four years ago were coming back into my mind. I started wondering about what was going to happen that night. Even though there'd been no calls and no signs that something was wrong, I couldn't completely let my suspicions go.

I figured they were probably clean but still had a thought or two that they might be with the federal government, that somehow we'd been found out. But there was no way in the world that anyone could have known what we were up to because of the safeguards we had set up, at least, that's what I kept telling myself.

When they pulled up to my house that night, I saw their name tags engraved with the name of their church and how young they were and it blew my mind. I later learned that one of them was just fresh out on his mission, that I was the first lesson he'd been a part of. So there they were in my house. Lynette was there, too. They'd asked to be able to talk to both of us.

Whenever I got nervous, I smoked Tiperillos. I was smoking that night but I could tell they were uncomfortable with it and stopped. I sat back and said, "Okay, tell me what you're all about."

I sat in my chair and I watched them real close as they started making their presentation. They had all these pictures, charts and stuff. They wanted to start off making small talk but I wouldn't let them. *Just get to it*, I thought.

I listened for a while as they talked about the lessons they had to teach and started with the church's belief in Jesus Christ and something they called the Plan of Salvation.

They talked about how we were all spirits together in Heaven before the earth was formed. They said God, or Heavenly Father as they called him, had given us a chance to come to earth to gain bodies and learn. There had been two plans given in Heaven, they said.

Jesus Christ believed the spirits should have the ability to make their own choices on earth to learn for themselves about God and one day be able to return to live with him. But Satan, the kids told us, had a different plan. He wanted to force everyone to do the right thing. There was some kind of battle between the spirits, with the followers of Jesus winning out. They would go to earth and have the ability to choose for themselves. The Mormons believed that Jesus died so that people could be forgiven of the things that they did wrong and be able to go back to live with Heavenly Father after they died.

The two missionaries hadn't gotten far into their lesson when I stopped them short. I started asking questions. I was shooting them all over the board because they were supposed to have all this information. I was asking them "You're supposed to know so much, so tell me about this earth, why are we here?"

I wanted to hear what they would say because no one had

ever been able to give me the right answers. So one of the missionaries opened some scriptures he had and laid it all out.

He showed me the book, called the Book of Mormon, and started reading me passages that seemed to answer my questions head on. I hadn't heard of the book before but I didn't have a problem with it.

I had never really read the Bible so this was just another kind of scripture to me. But what he was reading was making sense. That was the most flabbergasting thing about the whole evening—that what these guys were saying was *really* making sense. They were giving me answers to questions that I had been looking for, for years and years, throughout my whole lifetime, really.

That's why I never got along with the Catholic Church because the priest always said, "You just do what we want you to do and don't worry about anything else." That never clicked with me because they were talking about this wonderful God that I'm supposed to have faith in but I knew I was listening to a priest who was saying one thing and doing another.

So I was riveted by the discussion going on in my home that night. I kept asking questions and they kept coming up with answers using the Book of Mormon and the Bible, too.

The time flew by and it was 10 P.M. They had to leave, they said. They would be very happy to come back another time but they had rules. They had to get home. "No," I told them. "If you leave now, don't come back."

I was wrapped up in it. They were answering the questions and I wanted to keep going. They insisted they had to go, that they had someone called a mission president who set these rules and who they had to answer to.

"Get him on the phone," I said. They looked at each other like, "Whoa, we can't do that," but I told them if they wanted to come back they'd better get him on the phone.

The missionary who was making the call was really nervous but he picked up the phone and made the call anyway. I talked to the mission president myself.

"I know the boys have rules and stuff but I enjoy listening to what they have to say," I told the faceless person on the other end. "I don't want to wait another week. I'll see that they get home safely so you don't have to worry about it."

The president wasn't easily convinced. He brought up these rules that they were expected to stick to. But I wouldn't listen.

"If they can't stay now, don't bother sending them back," I said.

I meant it, too. He finally agreed, telling me to tell the one missionary to call him when they got back later that night. I told him again I'd make sure they got back with no problem.

My reasons for wanting them to stay were real, but my insistence on seeing that they got home safe would pay an extra dividend. I still had a niggling doubt in my mind about what they were all about, so I figured I'd find out where they lived if I ever needed to know that information.

So the discussions went on. They kept referring to the Book of Mormon, opening to certain sections and, at one point, started asking me to read them out loud. One missionary starting pushing me to read and I got really nervous.

"Why don't you read this?" he'd ask.

"No, you read it," I said each time. The other missionary picked up on my reluctance, figured that I probably couldn't read or wasn't good at it, and so they backed off on that part.

I finally noticed they were getting tired, but I wasn't ready to let them go. We went through about four of their lessons, getting to a part about donations to their church that the members were expected to make. They called it tithing. That discussion got hot and heavy.

The Catholics bring in all this money and I was suspicious of any church asking for money. These missionaries were telling me how it went back into their church to build churches, help the hungry and all that. I asked them to prove that and he explained all the accounting, the ward budgets, how it was laid out and that intrigued me, being a business guy and all.

But I wanted to get back to knowing about the Lord, so the missionaries started talking about some guy named Joseph Smith. I'd never heard of him.

Now once they started talking about this young boy who prayed and saw God and Jesus and found a buried gold book, I got really skeptical. That was the low point of the evening.

I wondered, if after all these hours, had I just been conned by these two guys?

Whenever I feel like I was being played by anyone in any situation, I always clam up and start listening real close. That's what I did that night, looking for signs of unsteadiness.

But there was nothing but consistency in what these two were saying. They didn't vary one bit and they were very sincere. They just kept doing their thing. There wasn't any cover-up. There wasn't any apologizing for what they knew must sound kind of far-fetched to a guy like me. They were just like, "This was the first modern-day prophet of the church."

As they continued, I loosened up enough to ask more questions. This went on until 2 A.M. when I finally let them leave. But I followed them home. I jumped in my car to make sure they'd be okay like I'd said I would and reminded them about calling their boss.

And we made an appointment for the next week.

T E N

As each day passed since that marathon visit, my mind was preoccupied with everything I'd heard, what those young boys had to say. It was really working on me. It was like whispers, voices, reminders following me around that wouldn't let me forget.

All this was going on in my head and I couldn't talk to anybody about it, especially not the people I was involved with. It wasn't because of the nature of our dealings but because to them, religion was one of the most successful scams of all time— a front used to draw in millions and millions of dollars.

Why was I thinking about this stuff at all? What was a guy like me doing, making my own fortune on the wrong side of the law, letting his mind be filled with questions about religion, God, some prophet named Joseph Smith and a church I'd only barely heard of two weeks earlier?

Maybe it was because when you have all you need to sustain your life and all the toys you ever wanted, constantly driving for more and more, you come to a point where you start saying to yourself, "What's the purpose of all this?" The purpose I had was to get as much for myself as I could. It was a game. And it was a fun game.

But that whole week I felt like there was someone who was following me around, whispering in my mind, "Do you think what they said is right?" I was battling with my mind all through those days thinking about tithing, prophets, the reason for life and all that.

Lynette had sat through the first meeting, but I could tell she wasn't that interested. In fact, she kept falling asleep. She was there because I was there. And she liked the kids because they were polite, nice and respectful—characteristics she wasn't used to seeing in kids that age. It was a pleasure to have them in our home.

The second time they came over, she was waiting with me again. If I was there, she was there, too. It didn't take long before we were back in deep, discussing the Book of Mormon and Joseph Smith and, to my dismay, requests that I read aloud some of the passages. About halfway through, I took the one missionary aside.

"I need to talk to you," I said. "I know you know I don't know how to read so do me a favor and quit asking me. You're embarrassing me."

He got real red in the face, saying, "Okay, okay. I won't, I won't."

So we went back inside and we discussed a lot about Joseph Smith. We spent a lot of time talking about him before they said they wanted to show us a movie. I think it was called *Families are Forever.* It was all about families, and that hit me because I grew up in a big family. I listened as they talked about Heavenly Father and the focus on families in their church.

When that was over, we got back to talking about Joseph

Smith. The whole thing was kind of hard to swallow, I mean, Heavenly Father coming out of the sky with Jesus to a guy named Joseph Smith. If I told that to the guys I knew, they'd be sure I was crazy. But I listened . . . I really honestly listened to what these missionaries were saying.

I paid even closer attention when they explained to me about what they were about. How they volunteered to go on a mission at age nineteen, paying for it themselves. I had asked how much they were getting paid and they started telling me about the missionary program. And that just totally rocked me back.

Why would anybody take their own time, especially when they were so young and all that, to go somewhere they'd never been without being paid . . . and here these kids, were taking two years of their lives to teach the gospel; that made me pay attention.

The lesson was only four hours that night, but as they left I asked if they wanted me to follow them home again. I went outside with them and one of the missionaries went to the trunk of their car, opened it, and gave me a Book of Mormon.

"You try to read this," he told me, handing me a copy. "If you read it the first time, you'll be able to read anything after that."

I stared back at him. "Man, I never went past the tenth grade," I said. "I bluffed my way through school up to the tenth grade. I don't think I can do it."

"Get on your knees and pray about it," the missionary responded.

Earlier in the lesson, they'd taught me about praying. I had never known how to do that before. It was always just the sign of the cross and repeating some prayer written by someone else a long time ago.

So they wrote down the order of prayer for me. First you address Heavenly Father, they said. Next, I was supposed to say the things I was thankful for in my life before asking for specific blessings. The prayer was to be closed in the name of

Jesus Christ. They told me that if I asked Heavenly Father for help and I started reading the Book of Mormon, that I'd be able to read.

I heard that and was saying to myself, *You mean, all I've got to do is just get on my knees and follow this order and ask and I'll be able to start reading?*

I found that difficult to believe. So the missionary gave me a challenge and I jumped on it.

I decided to pray but didn't do it in front of my wife, though. She thought the missionaries and their church were nice, but she didn't really get into it. She went to bed and I stayed in the living room, opened the Book of Mormon and started looking at it.

I saw the words, the sentences, the unfamiliar language of a time long ago and the doubts flooded my mind. So I got on my knees there by the couch in the living room. I was nervous. I wasn't embarrassed, but I was very nervous because, what if there really *was* a God?

I was so used to conning people and wondered if I was being conned. Or, alternately, was I conning God? If there was a God. I got on my knees and I looked at this piece of paper the missionary gave me. "Address our Heavenly Father, then you thank him," he wrote. "Then ask him and then close."

"Okay," I thought. "I can do this." So I tried it. No big deal. I mean, I just asked to be able to read. I went to bed for the night, uncertain that the words had gone any further than the walls of the living room.

It was Saturday the next morning, and there was plenty of yard work to do and stuff to get to at the office. So I went in, taking the book with me. I was by myself. I sat behind my desk and opened up this book. I was looking at it and, line by line, read the introduction to it. I was there about three hours reading just the front part of it.

The missionary had explained to me a little bit about what took place in the Book of Mormon, the history and that it was the most correct book that had ever been written. That intrigued me . . . that claim intrigued me.

I was reading about a page an hour and comprehending it. Before this, I could take a magazine that had something about trucks and by myself I could sit and slowly read out, "The truck has power brakes" haltingly as I stumbled through each word. But then I would get to a big word, get stuck and then lose interest in it because I got all bent out of shape in frustration.

So what I was doing with the Book of Mormon was going word by word and the more I got into it, the more it felt like everything was making sense.

I didn't get bored. It was hard and sometimes it was frustrating because some words I didn't understand. But I didn't get bored.

So, I kept reading.

ELEVEN

We went to a Mormon church meeting for the first time on a 4th of July weekend, a little more than a month since those boys had come to our door.

I was very curious to see what the meeting would be like but Lynette was kind of scared. I had nothing to be scared of. I had everything I wanted, so no one could do anything to me that'd make me worry.

I went to what the Mormons called a Sacrament meeting for the first time and I couldn't believe what I saw, or rather, what I didn't see. There were no bells ringing. No one was throwing smoke around. No big white clothes. Nobody dressed in robes. The clergy wasn't paid, I had already been told that, but they were actually members from the congregation called upon to fill certain roles in the church. Everyone could and would have the chance to serve somehow.

These young boys were serving their sacrament—bits of bread and tiny cups of water—and everything was just all so nice and organized. I got good vibes, good feelings about it. That day was something called "Fast and Testimony" meeting. On that day, I was told, members were asked to go without food for two meals to sacrifice, to overcome their physical needs and also to be closer to their Heavenly Father's spirit.

At that meeting, they said, anyone in the audience who wanted to, could come forward to express their feelings about the church, their testimonies of its truthfulness. I found it very interesting. I heard the people saying over and over, "I know this church is true."

I wondered to myself, "How do they know this? What, did God come down and say, 'Hey, Joe, this is the true church'?"

Things were just rushing through my mind while I was there.

I was introduced to the head of the congregation who is called a bishop. Bishop Gerald Duncan was a unique man. He had discernment. He could see right through me. He looked me square in the eye as we looked at each other. He smiled, took about three steps back from me and said, before turning to greet someone else, "We'll talk."

That concerned me a little. I wondered why he had said that, what he meant. The missionaries knew nothing of my livelihood; they were totally in the dark. They knew I had a trucking business but that was the extent of it.

I didn't give the comment a whole lot more thought and went home, impressed with what I had seen and experienced and ready to learn more.

By the time the missionaries arrived at the house for their third visit, I was making good progress (for me) through the Book of Mormon.

After they'd shown us the movie about families, I'd asked if they had anything else like that. When they told me there were numerous film titles, I asked them to bring one each time. I continued to be fascinated, intrigued by this religion.

On the next visit, the missionaries brought a film about the dedication of the Washington, D.C. temple. We talked a bit more about the Book of Mormon and then I set up the movie screen.

The missionaries started telling me about temples. When they described them to me and what their purpose was, the image of the Salt Lake temple popped into my mind. When they showed me a picture of the Washington D.C. temple, it reminded me of the Salt Lake temple, so I told them how I'd seen it on my trip and how impressed I was by it.

They showed me the movie about the dedication of the Washington, D.C. temple. It showed the construction of this magnificent towering building outside the capital, crowned by a golden statue of the Angel Moroni.

Moroni, I'd already learned, was an ancient prophet who had lived on the American continent and who had been responsible for burying the golden plates of recorded writings that in the nineteenth century became the Book of Mormon.

The narrator in the video explained the Mormon belief in the Plan of Salvation. We can all live again with our Heavenly Father and our families if we believe in Jesus Christ and follow his commandments, the voice continued.

Inside the temple building were sealing rooms where brides and grooms could get married, not just until death when they would part, but for eternity. If they kept the promises they made in the temple, they and their future children would never be separated, even by death.

Mormons believed in doing baptisms by proxy, inside the temple, for those who had died. This would give those spirits the opportunity to accept Christ's gospel in the hereafter and be reunited with their family members in Heaven one day.

The narrator continued as the camera looked inside the temple, captured some of the dedicatory service and finally, hoisted aloft by a helicopter, circled the spires including the one topped by the glistening, golden figure of Moroni holding his trumpet aloft into the sky.

That just penetrated me. It sent volts of electricity running through me. Just looking at that statue, and knowing what he represented and what it was all about, it blew me away.

Something inside me broke open. I bawled like a baby.

It was just this feeling that I had to get into that building. I could not explain the feeling. In the film, when they were interviewing people after the dedication, waves of good feelings came over me.

When the lights came back up, I turned to those boys and said, "I have to go to that building. What do I have to do to get there?"

I knew what I saw was right. There wasn't any doubt in my mind that what they'd shown to me was true, was meant to be. I knew it was right.

I started pounding them with questions about the temple, really getting on them. That's a bad habit I have. When I really want to know about something, I don't stop until I find out about it. I want to know now!

They explained to me that I would have to wait for a year after being baptized to be able to go inside because I would need that time to learn more and become ready to make even more commitments there.

The first step, they said, was to become a member of the church.

"Let's go do it," I said.

The younger missionary about fell off of his chair. The other said, "Whoa, there's still more lessons to teach."

From that point on, I knew. I knew what I had been hearing from these missionaries was true. I knew I had to join this church; I had to get to that temple. So, as impatient as I was to be baptized, I scheduled the rest of the lessons for the coming weeks.

One night the missionaries took me to a fireside, an evening meeting where church speakers talk to an audience on a specific topic or two. It was held at the mission home—the headquarters of the mission in Detroit.

That night I met President Bruce Talbot for the first time, the guy I'd talked to on the phone that first night the missionaries came by—the boss who had finally given in and let the elders continue their lessons into the early morning hours.

He looked right at me, right square in the eyes, like Bishop Duncan had done. We talked about the lessons, the missionaries, the church. He never took his eyes off of me. I felt like he was getting into my brain. I felt a little funny, a bit taken aback.

After the fireside, we went to a little room in the building. I knew I had to have an interview with the mission president before I would be allowed to be baptized and become a member of the Mormon church. I wasn't sure what to expect.

"I understand you want to be baptized," he said.

"Yes, I do," I responded. "I just feel good about what these boys are telling me."

"You know," he said mysteriously, "there's probably a lot more reasons why you aren't being baptized than why you are. Give me a few days and I'll let you know."

A couple days later he called saying I had permission to be baptized.

I failed to see the conflict between my business dealings and this new religion. Bishop Duncan and President Talbot both interviewed me prior to the baptism date in September. But I didn't divulge anything beyond the typical story of how I made a living and then we discussed my feelings about the things the missionaries had taught.

It never really crossed my mind that the two didn't mesh. That's because that's the way Catholics, or at least this Catholic, were brought up. You could be Joe Willie Hitman as long as you gave $1,000 a month to the church. Because you still believe in God and you go to confession and confess your sins—everything's square. That was the thought I'd always had.

I figured I could just treat this new religion like everyone I knew treated the Catholic Church.

Boy, did I figure it wrong.

T W E L V E

Dressed in white and seated next to Lynette, who also wore white, I listened as the speaker talked about being baptized by immersion in water, about starting a new life with a clean slate before God.

Gathered in a Mormon church near our home were the two of us, the missionaries, members of the ward and others who would participate in or witness what Mormons believe is the first essential step to returning to their Heavenly Father.

With the image of the temple still burning in my head, I knew I was making the right choice. Lynette, well, she was there because I was there, just like always. But my mind was mainly on myself and my goal of getting to that temple someday.

I stepped into the baptismal font along with one of the missionaries who had first come to our house that day, just a few months earlier, and he baptized me a member of The Church of Jesus Christ of Latter-day Saints, immersing me in the water to complete the ordinance. Lynette followed as I watched, still dripping from my own baptism.

After Lynette and I had dried off and changed, there was another talk, this one about someone called the Holy Ghost, someone we had learned about in our earlier discussions with the missionaries. He was the third member of the Godhead along with Heavenly Father and Jesus Christ. We had earlier learned and accepted that the Godhead was made up of three separate beings; not just one entity as the Catholics thought. A spirit being, the Holy Ghost was to be a constant companion, a comforter, a voice whispering promptings when I was faced with difficult choices.

At the time, I thought the concept was great; I had no clue about the difficult choice I was soon to face, no idea at all.

One after the other, Lynette and I each sat in a chair in front of the gathering as several of the men in the church, including the missionaries, placed their hands on our heads. Mormons believe in a priesthood, a literal power given to worthy men to act in God's name. It is through that power that we were baptized and now, confirmed members of His church. One of these men said a blessing, confirming us members of the church and giving us the gift of the Holy Ghost for as long as we kept ourselves worthy to receive his help. He also asked the Lord for many things on our behalves before concluding the prayer. I knew what I had just done was right. No doubts at all.

It was like I was back in that play, in that dream I'd had in Provo just last spring, where I finally was taking the right road. And I had finally gone down the yellow brick road.

I really thought about that dream. I was sure now, that it was a prompting of things to come, a warning to take the chance to change my course when it presented itself at my doorstep. Only later, did I realize I'd only just reached the fork in the road; the true change in direction was yet to come.

Watching the baptisms and confirmations in that church that

day were several men, including the bishop and the president of the stake, a larger demographic region of Mormon congregations, along with several others who were professionals in their fields and avid scriptorians.

I wondered why they were there at my baptism. They were very distinguished, and they all stood out in my mind because they were very concerned, making sure everything was done correctly.

The day was memorable and extremely meaningful for me.

Baptism brought changes, but not the ones that should have seemed the most obvious.

The Mormons have a health code they refer to as the Word of Wisdom. Members are counseled not to smoke, drink alcohol or coffee, eat a lot of meat or anything else in excess. It is basically just common sense health guidelines, but a member must follow them if they want to enter the temple.

And I did . . . no question.

The coffee was a little tough because I used to drink a cup of coffee every morning, but giving it up was no drastic thing. Drinking was no big deal. I had never been a heavy drinker, always wanting to be alert, on my toes.

Then there was tithing. That meant donating ten percent of what I made to the church. I paid tithing but not on all the money I was bringing in. But my wife had a problem with the tithing principle. We really fought over that big time, some of the biggest arguments I ever had with her. She didn't like the idea of dishing all that money out. I was giving $300, $400 a week from my regular salaries and business, the up-front stuff that I was doing. She didn't like that.

Nor was she enthusiastic about attending church meetings weekly. But it wasn't a problem for me, I went to church every Sunday. The reason Lynette was always uneasy about church every week was because she didn't like meeting separately with the women church members during a time period called Relief Society. She didn't like what she called a "goody two-shoes" attitude she thought she found there.

We had come off the street, never been members before and, of course, the curious kept an eye on us as we went to classes, met with people. They were helpful in getting us familiar with what went on each Sunday and that was their job. But Lynette thought everyone had this attitude and was out of touch with reality. That's not how I saw it. I liked coming to church because every Sunday I learned something. And I was hungry to learn. It was just exciting to get to the building each week, wondering what new thing I would learn, what new insight into my life and its purpose I could gain. It was something I looked forward to.

The missionaries continued to visit the house, teaching us lessons intended for new members, but again I bowled them over with questions, messing up their lesson plans, getting the answers I was looking for. I had read the Book of Mormon before I'd been baptized and I continued to read afterwards. Sometimes, I would read something that just wouldn't click so I'd throw it at the missionaries or at those smart professional guys at church.

I was reading every day. I was driven to know more and more. Everything made so much sense. You hear so many things about religion when you're growing up as a kid, all that hearsay, all the malarkey and stuff, and then all of a sudden you're reading things that make sense.

I mean, this Book of Mormon stuff could really have happened. *This is something,* I thought as I read another account from the book. *There's no way this could be fiction.*

It was reality. Every time I read three, four chapters, I'd sit there and think about it and try to do what the prophet of the church had said, to ponder what I had just read.

That's what I was doing but I was also playing a game in my head. I put myself in the position of Abinadi, an ancient American prophet in the Book of Mormon, who entered the court of the wicked King Noah to try and call him to repentance. I imagined this skinny guy standing out there in front of this powerful king and his servants and I'd think, *boy, he had guts.*

He stood there and testified of the Lord and they killed him, I said in my head, contemplating the scene. I did that over and over as I read, trying to put myself in the situation of the person I was reading about. I was already in King Noah's position. I didn't have to put myself there. That wasn't hard to imagine at all. But just thinking of what Abinadi went through and then dying for it . . . that got me.

In the Book of Mormon, these prophets stand there and they testify of the church with such firm conviction. The spirit is undeniably there with them and nobody can stop them.

After Abinadi does what he was asked by the Lord to do, he just stands there and says, "Okay. I said what I had to say. Now you can do whatever you have to do to me. I don't care."

That to me was so amazing and the more I read about him, the more I drove one certain church member crazy. He was an expert on the scriptures and he patiently listened to my questions and managed to answer them to my satisfaction—no small task.

He'd told me to call him anytime. So I did. At work. At 2 A.M. Whenever my mind was questioning. He'd give me things to look up, to find my own answers and I did.

For the first three months that I was member, that was my focus—diving into the Book of Mormon. I found it very exciting and almost addictive.

I had to learn more.

THIRTEEN

Just as no one at Church knew of my business dealings, no one in the organization knew I had become a Mormon. There was no need for one to be aware of the other, as far as I was concerned.

I was extremely happy in this new church that challenged my mind and finally gave me the answers no one else had ever been able to provide to my satisfaction before. Work continued to go well, be profitable and carry on as always. New deals, new scams, working the old ones. Life was pretty good . . . or so I thought.

I didn't realize it yet, but I was changing. It wasn't too many months after I was baptized that I found out that some people I worked with had noticed I was behaving differently. They started asking questions.

I wasn't as hotheaded as I'd always been. I was getting a

little more cautious about the deals I set up or got involved in. "Should we really do that?" I found myself asking my partners.

It wasn't a conscious thing, it was just happening. And my partners were getting more and more curious about what was going on with me.

I'd been a member about four months when Bishop Duncan came up to me one Sunday during church as I walked down a hallway.

"After Sacrament meeting, I want to talk with you," he said.

"Sure," I responded, thinking it was no big deal.

So when the meeting ended, I was out visiting with some of the other members as they filtered out of the chapel. The bishop came up to me, put his arm around my shoulder and said, "Come with me."

So I did.

We went into his office and he shut the door . . . and locked it. What he said next about knocked me over, I was shocked.

"I don't know what you're doing or how you're doing it but you can't serve two masters," Bishop Duncan said, staring deep into my eyes. "Get rid of one. You must make that choice."

I was stunned. My heart went "boom" because I knew exactly what he meant. I had to stop what I was doing.

I just looked at him. "That's my living," I said. "How can I?"

"Well, you can't be a member of the church and make your living the way you are," he replied. He told me it had to be one or the other.

I was a nervous wreck. He had said what he intended to say and the meeting was over. I was so jolted by the exchange that I left before services were over. I was beside myself.

I did not want to leave behind the Mormon church just when I had found it. I was so at peace with myself and I was learning so much, gathering new knowledge and making new friends.

I just went home and I sat there . . . and sat there some more.

I knew I really needed to do some soul-searching, to think about the choice that had been laid out plainly in front of me.

After telling my associates I had to go up north for a few days, I headed toward a cabin I had that no one knew about. I wanted to get away, to be by myself, and really consider the situation I found myself in. I was making so much money, I wanted for nothing. The decision might have been easy for another guy, but not for me.

I had so invested myself, my whole soul, in this newfound religion that the thought of separating myself from it was almost unbearable. I had found answers that made sense, that gave my mind peace, that felt right. Could I give that up now, even with all the money at stake? And if I did, how likely was it that I would live to continue being a member of the Church here on earth?

All alone in that cabin I thought and I prayed, and I prayed and thought some more. It was me and Heavenly Father, talking it out. And it was me and myself wrestling with a decision I'd never imagined I'd face. Giving up all the worldly stuff, the money, the toys, and power; that was a tough decision. And even if I were willing to do that, how would I? How *could* I?

How was I going to tell the organization that I was not going to do this anymore? They'd kill me. I knew it. You don't just quit. There was no question of that. I had grown up knowing that. I knew it when I got involved, when the love of the scam drew me in. It didn't concern me then. It was a way of life, a very lucrative way of life that I couldn't foresee ever wanting to give up.

And now I did.

It all played back in my mind. The dream I'd had in that Provo hotel room. The bizarre decision by my wife to give the missionaries that secret number, something that forced me to meet them and talk to them. Watching the movie about the temple. The force of my reaction. The stilted prayer asking for help in reading the Book of Mormon. The peace I felt when I came out of the baptismal waters. The exhilaration of growing in knowledge. The wonder at the faith and courage of prophets like Abinadi.

There really was no choice, I finally concluded. I could not give it up.

From that point on, my life became focused on one final deal, one final objective that carried more risk that any ever before—how to get out of the organization with my life.

How could I do it and keep breathing?

I just figured I was a dead man.

I went back home and called Bishop Duncan and arranged a meeting.

"I want to stay in the Church," I told him. "There's no question of that."

I didn't tell him everything, but I tried to clue him in somewhat to the situation I faced.

"Look, if I walk away from this and tell them I want out, they'll kill me," I said bluntly. "Guys don't walk away from this."

He sat there, looked at me, and began shaking his head. "Don't you have any faith?" he asked.

"Well, yeah," I responded. "But you don't know my circumstances."

He paused briefly.

"There's nothing in your circumstances that you have to worry about," he said as I sat in disbelief. "So what if you get killed?"

I knew what he meant. Death would only bring me a step closer to a reunion with my Heavenly Father and Jesus Christ. It would not be a tragedy, but a progression in my eternal journey. Still, it was one I was reluctant to take just yet.

"But I haven't had a chance to get into the temple yet," I said back to him.

"You can only serve one master," he repeated.

I knew he was right, and I knew what I had to do. I impressed upon him that the things we had talked about, the things I had revealed to him, had to remain confidential.

"I don't want nothing coming back to the Church," I said, concerned for the possible fallout from my coming actions.

"Don't worry about that," he said. "Nothing will go further than this room." We both agreed the stake president should be filled in, however, and met with him at his earliest convenience.

I explained the circumstances and the crossroads I faced. "It's your choice," the stake president said, telling me what I already knew. "You have to make that choice. We can't make it for you."

I knew it would take time to work out the details and figure out my best chance of leaving with my life. I asked if I would still be able to attend church while I was making those arrangements. I could come, the two leaders told me, but I was not to take the Sacrament. That hurt. Not being allowed to participate in taking the bread and water was like saying, "We got you in a corner, baby. You've got to make a choice or out the window you go."

If I did manage to get out of the business without dying, what kind of life would I have, I wondered. *I was just some street kid with no real formal education or training. Without the organization, the connections I had there, what would I have, where would I be?*

I knew the trucking business, but if I got out of the organization, those guys weren't going to let me keep doing that. They'd stop me in a second. If I survived and they threw me out on the street, how was I going to make a living? Anything I could do, they had a connection with or controlled.

I was done. I knew it.

F O U R T E E N

My choice had been made.

It started an irreversible chain of events that could end with my mortal life being lost, and I knew it. But the conversations with the church leaders, those days alone in the cabin, the long prayerful hours, had made the situation perfectly clear.

I knew what I had been doing for a living, for a lifestyle, was wrong, very wrong. There was no longer any doubt about it. It was completely opposite to the teachings of Jesus Christ and his church, the church I had joined and embraced with such passion. It now was so clear, I couldn't believe I hadn't spotted the conflict myself, immediately.

Other than the bishop and stake president, no one knew of the inner torment and conflict of the decision I faced. Lynette never really knew all that I was up to anyway but she knew it wasn't exactly legitimate. And now she knew nothing of my discussions with the bishop, my wrenching days at the cabin and the life-altering if not life-ending choice, I'd made.

She never wanted to know the details of my businesses, just so long as the money kept coming in. Lynette had never even been overly concerned about that, never seemed like some kind of gold digger until we joined the church and I started putting so much in an envelope each week. Then she started questioning every cent.

We'd continued to battle about tithing and, as weeks passed, we battled about the church in general, too. She never had really believed it in the first place and things started getting worse between us. It was becoming part of my daily life, changing how I acted, but she was the same. We drifted farther apart as her resentment grew to my growing commitment to this church.

There was no way I would tell her what I was about to do. I knew it was going to take time to set things up if I wanted to have the best possible chance of living to go to the temple one day.

So I did the Jekyll and Hyde thing, continuing at work, struggling to be the same old Mario, the guy they could count on, the mastermind of some of the operation, the low-key one who kept things going on his end.

I had to be real careful, really careful all the time. I struggled with what I was going to do, how to get out, for about two months. I tried to piece it together, how I could make it all work. Finally, I reached a point where I figured I had to make a move. I was ready to do it.

I headed back to the cabin for another weekend, spending most of it in prayer.

"Lord," I appealed. "I want to do this. Just give me some direction of how to get out of this mess." I didn't ask for anything in particular. I just left it in His hands.

"Whatever you want me to do, I'll do it," I said in prayer over and over again. "However you think it's best, so be it."

Once I returned home, I finally began putting all the pieces together. I went to the garage at the office and pulled out the bundles of cash I'd stashed there in the pipe. At the very least, I thought, I'll have this money . . . if I even have my life when this is all over.

I told Lynette to go stay with her mother for a few days. She thought some kind of deal must be going on at the house and didn't give it another thought.

When everyone had cleared from the office one day, I took everything I knew I needed. I took documents, records, other items that would offer me some degree of protection once I made my intentions known to my bosses. These were the fellows who'd brought me up in the organization, who'd relied on my smarts to make them millions over the years.

The stash of paperwork went into a locker at Detroit Metropolitan Airport. I couldn't put them any place else because my pals would be able to track them down. The key firmly in my hand, I knew I could leave the papers there for up to several weeks and no one would be the wiser. They wouldn't be found until I was ready to reclaim them.

I left the pillowcase stuffed with rolls of bills, about $300,000 in laundered money, with a trusted friend as I made my final arrangements.

With Lynette safely away and the items I needed out of the office, the time had come to make my move. I made the call.

I was done, I said. I wanted out. There was no chance for further explanation. They went berserk. They couldn't believe what they were hearing.

"Just think about it," I said calmly. "I'll call back in a week or so."

After six days at my cabin, I drove north to Fort Mackinac to call them again. I called on a Saturday morning because I knew where they would all be meeting.

"Where are you?" they demanded to know. "Where is this record?" they insisted. "Where is that document?" they angrily asked. I knew the only thing that would save me were the piles of documents I had hidden away at the airport right before I left.

"Look," I said. "I'll give you what you want. I just want to make a deal with you."

"No deals. No deals," they said, getting increasingly hostile. That conversation ended when I told them I'd call back in a few days.

I returned to that same Fort Mackinac party store a week or so later, called them up again and said I was headed home.

"Look, I'm coming down," I told the guy on the other end. "I want to talk to Mr. Borilla, Let's put this thing to bed. I'll make a deal with you. I've got something on my mind and we'll go from there."

They were much calmer this time. They needed to see me, to know what I was up to, so they agreed to a meeting. They set the time. I knew the place.

I hung up the phone and headed back to the cabin. I collected my things, oddly at peace, as I began a drive that could be one of my last.

At the appointed time, I arrived at a warehouse in Detroit we used for storage. There was nothing spooky about it. Nothing that indicated the nature of the business it was used for, or the building tension of what was about to go down inside.

Everyone was waiting for me and the air was thick with anger, suspicion, and uncertainty. The big guys were especially anxious. They didn't know what was going on with me. They didn't know what I might have done, how far I might have gone, who I might have ratted to, who might be right behind me.

All they knew is that I all of a sudden got religion of some kind. Had I run to the FBI and spilled my guts? They must have wondered. Were they already doomed? Did I still have the documents? Had I lost my mind, thinking I could walk away?

All these unsaid fears were swirling around as I walked into the warehouse. There, seated by a small table, was the main guy, the man. All around were guys with guns, milling around, watching me closely as I made my way to the table and my destiny. I figured it was curtains for me, the end. I figured I'd never walk out of there.

I paused briefly, stumbling through a quick prayer in my head as suspicious eyes bored into me, trying to penetrate me from every angle.

"Whatever happens, happens," I quietly told the Lord.

"It's in your hands now."

FIFTEEEN

"What the hell is going through your mind?" Mr. Borilla barked at me as I approached the table where he waited. "What the hell are you thinking?"

"Well, I've joined this church," I started to say before he cut me off. He started peppering me with questions about the deals I was involved with, the documents I had in my possession, my roles in various operations.

"What did you do with this?" he asked about one operation. "What are you doing with that?" he demanded about another.

I sat and explained each deal to him, where it was and how I'd been running it. I already had planned out what I would tell them, how they could go on very successfully without me.

The knowledge I had was crucial to them. We were scamming, using several businesses to launder money, a lot of money. Big bucks . . . millions.

Things were going on that were mind boggling, but they didn't know the details of the operation and I did. They knew they were somewhat in the dark and that made them concerned. They were used to having all this money flowing from one place to the other; cash dollars in bags and suitcases. Here I was, a key to much of it, saying I wanted out. They looked at it as possibly losing millions of dollars in income, aside from the risk that I might flip to the feds, if I hadn't already.

In the midst of this barrage of questioning, I looked straight at him.

"Look, I don't want anything from you," I said.

He stared back at my eyes. "You mean you'd give everything up?"

"I don't need anything. I'll give it *all* up," I replied, concentrating only on him and not the glaring eyes of our associates. "I don't want anything," I assured him again, trying to convince him of my sincerity. "I just want to be left alone, and I just want to stay with my church."

"What is this church?" he asked.

"Have you heard of the Mormons?" I said, realizing this was the most bizarre of circumstances.

His eyes lit up briefly and he sat there, looking at me without saying anything.

"Who are they?" somebody else asked.

So I briefly explained to him how I'd come to join the Mormon Church and what it stood for. I told him because of my new beliefs, I no longer could continue to be involved in these types of operations. I needed to get out.

"You mean to tell me that you're going to give up all this stuff because of this church?" he asked incredulously. "What happens if we kill you? What are you going to have then?"

"Well, the only thing I'll be sorry about is that I never got to go to the house of the Lord, to the temple," I responded as he shook his head in disbelief. "But other than that, I think I'll be okay on the other side."

He let loose with a tirade that would have wilted flowers or any other living thing. Clearly, I had completely lost my mind or so it seemed to him and, most likely, everyone else standing in that warehouse. Mario's lost it, they thought, he's gone over the edge of insanity.

This can't be the same guy we've dealt with all these years, the guy who set us up in heavy equipment, who let us use his place to decide the fate of others just like him, who either decided they could do it on their own or wanted out.

For sure, Mario knew what this would mean, yet here he was. What was going on?

Through the exchange of words, Mr. Borilla sat there watching me, listening to what I said, looking and looking at me.

"I heard of those people," he said, finally breaking his silence. "I know they're good people and they're trustworthy people. If you live the way they want you to live, I have nothing to worry about." He paused another minute, looking right at me once again.

"So, are you going to live the way they want you to live?" he challenged me.

"Well, I wouldn't be here if I didn't want to do that," I said, not sure what he was getting at.

More minutes passed.

"You turn everything over," he ordered at last. "You don't own nothing. All you have is your house. If you're lucky, you're going to have that."

He said he was still turning it over in his brain, deciding what to do with me. What was saving me from certain death was that I didn't have a record. The police didn't know about me to lean on me. Only the guys in the room knew what I was about. That was it. I had never been out there being a hotshot, a Gotti kind of guy.

"Okay, I'll stand up for you, but don't ever breath a word of anything to anybody," he warned, his tone deadly serious. "The only reason you're getting out is because no else knows you but us."

"Get out of here," he continued. "I don't ever want to see you again. Don't ever get involved with anything because you're done."

He shook his finger in front of my face. "We're going to watch you," he warned. "We'll be watching all the time."

I couldn't quite believe what I was hearing. I was going to get out. . . I was going to live.

Or was I? I really didn't know. Was I about to be the victim in their latest scam? Wouldn't it be ironic if slick Mario who always played the game so well lost in the final round?

As I listened to him go on about how I'd better watch myself, about how not one breath of what we'd been involved in better ever cross my lips, I wondered if I was being softened up, relaxed so I wouldn't see what was coming.

Maybe one of the guys was behind me, about to throw a rope around my neck. Or maybe the barrel of a gun was trained at my head. I didn't know. As I sat there, I felt the Lord had put me there, at that crossroad of my life, to see what I was made of, my own ordeal in the court of wicked King Noah.

"I want to see how much guts you've got," I imagined He was saying to me. I knew He was watching my every move too, listening to my every word as I explained about the Church and what it meant to me, to men who had the power to eliminate me.

"What are you going to do?" I could almost hear Him saying to me. "Are you going to fink out at the last minute or are you going to stand there and take it? Are you willing to have someone eliminate you?" I imagined Him asking me these questions, as I took the biggest gamble of my life.

But it wasn't really a gamble at all. If I ended up dead in that warehouse, I knew I would still go ahead with it. My parents would be devastated, I was sure, but I would have only one real regret—that I never made it to the temple. That thought really bothered me because I wanted more than anything to get inside at least once before my life was over. I knew I had to go there.

I had made a decision. I knew that the Church was true and I had to say those words in that warehouse, to that man. It had been made very clear to me in ways I could not have imagined. I knew it was right. There was no way in the world I could deny it. And there was no way I was going to turn my back on that.

"If that's the deal, I'll shake on it," I said trying not to sound too eager. A handshake would bind him. There could be no death under those terms.

"Okay," he said, "it's a deal." He offered his hand and I shook it. And with that shake, the others in the room—shocked beyond belief at what had transpired and certain I deserved to die—also were bound.

They could not go out on their own and do me in. That would violate the deal and they would be history as well. That's the kind of power this man had, and they knew it. But it didn't stop the threats.

"I'm going to bury you if it's the last thing I ever do," hissed one of the guys as I left. I knew he stood to lose a lot of money as I walked out of the building; he and I had been very tight on a deal. "You hear me?" he asked, his voice dripping with contempt.

With each footstep, I moved closer to the warehouse door, still not completely sure I wouldn't be taken out from behind before I reached it.

I made it out the door.

Nothing.

I made it to my car.

Still nothing.

I put my key in the ignition and started the engine, wondering what might be wired under the hood.

No explosion.

I pulled out of the lot and started driving down the road. At that moment, sweet relief and amazement poured over me. I realized that I had done the impossible, escaped from the mob with my life.

I didn't know what lay ahead. I had the money stashed away, a wife whom I was losing and no skills outside of industries I'd just been warned away from for the rest of my life.

My car hadn't traveled far down the road when I paused and said a prayer in my head.

"Heavenly Father, thank you," I said, uttering the most sincere words ever to cross my lips.

"Now, let's get to work."

S I X T E E N

I was one lucky son-of-a gun to get away from there. That thought kept playing over and over in my mind as I got further away from the warehouse—a place that could've been a setting for an execution order.

I had no doubt in my mind as to why my life was spared.

There was work for me left to do here on the earth. I had thought and thought about this as I'd waited out in the cabin all those days, going back and forth in my head about the confrontation facing me.

I realized that if the Lord needed me or knew He was going to need me, in some certain area to do a certain thing, He also knew I could find the strength to do what I needed to do—face possible death to free myself from the ties that would forever hold me back from the life I now believed was the only acceptable choice.

The Lord had a big part in this, I told myself. *This isn't any fluke.* The Lord said, "Hey, I need this guy and if it works out and he grabs a hold of the gospel, I'm going to make it work out for him."

And He made it work.

I know that's exactly how it happened because there isn't any other explanation for why I walked away. What would possess a man who could shoot me on the spot to tell me, "Oh, I've heard of those people and I know they're good so I have nothing to worry about"? Come on. There was no question who had intervened.

The deal was done. I had accomplished what I wanted to accomplish and now it was time to move on. Now, it was all about staying straight. I told myself that—I've got to do things right.

The businesses that I had, had some legitimate parts, nothing crooked, so I knew I could hang on to those. I had to walk away from the trucking business and that was tough because there was a lot of money that was invested in there. But I had to walk away from it, I had to sign everything over.

So I headed home and started laying the groundwork to tell my wife that I wasn't going to have the trucking business anymore.

A few days later I met with a few of the guys to sign over about everything I had. I was left with the cash they didn't know about, the house and two legitimate businesses. I figured I could still make a living because I had the cash to back me up. If I did my thing as far as the legitimate business was concerned, I'd be okay.

We signed the papers and I gave everything to them, which was part of the deal. I really didn't care about what I had to give up or sign away. I just figured they were letting me slide out; that was more than enough for me to think I'd got the good end of the deal.

It wasn't three weeks before I realized that the payment

had just begun. What I'd given up was not enough, not nearly enough for others in the group still enraged that I was out and still alive.

Out of nowhere I started getting sued by these guys. They alleged breach of contract. They said I'd borrowed money from the company. Another guy came out of the woodwork and said I owed him $25,000. He actually had a note typed up with my signature saying I owed him the cash.

How he did that, I don't know, but I wasn't surprised. I figure this was all done while I was signing those papers over. There must have been a carbon under some of the sheets I signed and when I did, it came through on this note or something like that. It was my signature. No doubt about it.

These guys were pulling the corks everywhere. They were really coming at me. I hired attorneys to try and fight the lawsuit and fight the fraudulent claim. I hadn't expected this. Two things I figured might come up, but the other attacks never occurred to me. I thought I was free and clear.

Just as everything started coming at me and I was shelling out all this money for attorneys, my marriage fell apart. I was back in court again, this time for a divorce.

Lynette and I, we'd had a mutually beneficial relationship. She was a valuable asset to some of the things I did, although she never knew much, just did what was asked, and, in turn, she never had to worry about money. We provided each other with companionship but didn't have the deep connection we should have had.

Now I was fighting for my livelihood *and* trying to maintain a standard of living I didn't have the cash to support. I was fighting to keep what money I had left. I always had had a lot of cash so we'd never worried about anything, as far as having the money for our needs. We bought stuff, took off on vacations, did what we wanted. The money was always there.

Our standard of living started to dive and I was concerned. Lynette now hated the Church because she believed it was to blame for our freefall from the good life. We began to have more and more differences over everything. The distance between us grew as I became even more involved in the Church and was learning more and more as I pursued my goal of going to the temple.

What I was really doing was trying to make right choices, to learn everything I could about the church and its teachings.

Lynette, she just wanted out. She didn't want to put up with going to Church every Sunday. It got worse as I started getting involved in church activities. So we filed for a divorce.

All the while, the court battles continued. Lynette's mother entered the mix, suing me and claiming I owed her $5,000. So I had to go to court and try to defend myself against all of this. She had checks that I had given her for $500 here, $800 there and she used those as evidence, saying I had really borrowed $10,000 but had paid back only half. Naturally Lynette was sitting there going, "Yup, yup, he got $10,000." So here I was battling back and forth and trying to stay strong in the church.

It didn't scare me though, I just got mad. It made me more determined that there was nothing that was going to sway me from the Church. They couldn't hurt me, none of them.

There was a deal that was made. When you make a deal, especially a deal with the Lord, you better live by the deal because somewhere down the line, if you don't, you're going to pay the price. I knew that.

But I also knew that the other deal I had, the one sealed that day in the warehouse, had its limits. I knew I couldn't just walk away from that life with no other consequence. He'd spared my life but he'd made no other deals. He just said, "We will not touch you as long as you keep your mouth shut." That was the deal.

I should have known better than to think the cash and the few business connections I had left would see me through financially as I tried to build a life that squared with the beliefs of the Church I'd joined.

Hey, I can walk away from this and still make a living, I'd figured. But the money I had stashed, the money I was counting on to pull me through, had been made illegally. But I wasn't smart enough to realize the Lord was going to have no part in protecting it or saving it for me.

I figured, *Well, I'm doing the right things now, so I don't have to worry.* But it wasn't that way. The Lord was telling me, "Hey, you've got bad money and here you're trying to survive with it" and I wasn't paying attention. I was praying for help but didn't listen for the answer.

So I learned the hard way. There was no heavenly intervention. Instead I was going to court, fighting these battles on my own, hamstrung because my pledge to keep quiet meant I couldn't tell my attorneys information they needed to know to defend me. I had to be careful what I said, with what I told them, because they couldn't know what was really going on and it was costing me thousands of dollars. They didn't have all the facts and I couldn't give them to them. And the other side knew it. Either way I lost, it was just a question of whether I'd pay in cash or with my life.

I had to be careful, very careful. On a few of the cases, I just threw up my hands and said, "Stuff it. I don't need this," and just let it go. There went $20,000 out the window here, $25,000 gone there.

Things at one of my remaining businesses had turned sour. Things just got worse and worse. I was getting resistance there because I was trying to suddenly become active in a company I really didn't know much about. And there were those inside who still were set on laundering money. It's still running today. So I threw up my hands with that business; gave the company over to them, signed it away.

It seemed every day someone new popped out of the woodwork with a new claim of something I owed them. I was fighting these people in court, fighting allegations that had no basis in reality. They showed up with all this trumped-up stuff.

They'd saved checks that I'd written out to guys for doing things but hadn't kept track of because we *couldn't* keep track of it. Any record was a potential bomb.

So I ate it all . . . everything. By the time my divorce was final, all $300,000 was gone. I ended up totally busted. I had kept paying tithing through it all, thinking, *Man, I'm doing the right thing here.*

There weren't too many people at church who knew what was going on as far as the divorce—only a handful. When it was clear the marriage was dead, I'd told Lynette to go ahead and get an attorney and work things out. I was consumed with the other court battles. Well, she and her lawyer did a slick job on me. They took me to the cleaners, and I didn't even pay attention because I didn't think she was going to be like that.

So I walked away from it totally broke. All I had was my car, my clothes, and ten or twelve dollars to my name. I had a little Ford and one house, which Lynette took. Here I was, a guy who'd used a Cadillac for a personal car, who drove a top-of-the-line pickup for work, with only a Ford for a car.

And now I didn't even have a place to live. I packed what I had left in the car and left the house.

Finally my old life was behind, but I was totally wiped out.

SEVENTEEN

That night I slept in the car. Already, I was planning my next move, putting a program together to try and get some stability back.

I figured I would have to go back to driving a truck because that was the best thing I knew how to do. The next day was Sunday and there was no question where I was headed. I knew a guy who let me stop by, take a shower, and put on my suit.

I was totally wiped out but off the top of my head I thought of some trucking companies that I knew that would hire me. Sure, I'd spent the night in the car but I had no doubt I could pull myself back up again. Of course, no one at Church knew what had happened to me. I walked in like it was any other Sunday.

A plastic surgeon who was a member of the congregation

approached me as I walked through the hall. He came up, put his arm around me, looked right at me and said, "Are you good at collecting money?"

"Yes," I answered, wondering what this was about. "What do you need?"

"I have more than $200,000 that patients owe me," he said, explaining he was looking for help in collecting the fees. "I'll pay you twenty-five percent of what you collect and I'll give you a weekly salary. Just show up tomorrow at my office."

I hardly knew what to say. I was completely blown away. This guy had no idea of the situation I was in and here he was just offering a job, out of the blue.

I had one asset left, the cabin up north. Nobody knew I had it and I had to get rid of it. I had no place to stay so I got in touch with this guy who I knew who was looking for a place up north. I went to his place Sunday night and talked with him until about 1:30 A.M., then told him I had to go. It was so late, he offered to let me stay.

I think he knew I was in a bad way. I'm sure he saw the clothes in my car. I sold that cabin not long after that but, like a bad scene that kept replaying, someone else came out of nowhere saying I owned him $25,000 and that ate up the rest of the money. I was done. Everything that I had ever had from before was gone. I joined the church and started over again from ground zero.

Just as I'd agreed, I went to the doctor's office the next morning. I asked him why he'd offered me the job.

"You've got the type of personality that people will listen to," he said. "You'll get the money if you lean on them."

He did a lot of plastic surgery on women and I couldn't believe the amount of money he had out on the street. He gave me all the files and put me in this small room with a phone and said, "Go to work."

He advanced me $500 so I was able to get a place to stay until my first paycheck came in. That Monday, I went to work and from then on, everything I did was up front and honest. I collected about $180,000 for the doctor so it was mutually beneficial although I was sure I was the real winner in the deal, given that I'd been looking at living in my car when the whole thing started.

It had been about eight months since I'd joined the church and my life was nothing like what it had been when I'd first met the missionaries. But the obsession I had to get to the temple, that was the same.

Now I started asking more questions of members, of leaders. I started leaning on the bishop. I started taking classes on going to the temple. The teacher was really, really good with me, patient with my endless stream of questions. I really was possessed, wanting badly to do the work.

I heard people talk about the temple, and seeing those pictures I had an idea in my mind of what I thought it was like. I went through the whole process to get ready to go. The days until I was eligible couldn't go fast enough for me.

By then I'd gotten an apartment in Wixom and still was working for the doctor but I'd taken on two or three other things on the side. I was getting by. I went to the bishop and the stake president to get interviewed for my recommend, the final hurdle to being able to walk through those temple doors. After all those months, it was finally within my reach. I knew I could honestly say I paid a full tithing, intended to live according to even greater covenants with the Lord and, finally, was honest in all my dealings with others.

The ward was planning a big trip to the Washington, D.C. temple, some twelve hours away, and there was no way I was going to miss it. Once I'd had my interviews, I talked to the bishop about the plans for the trip.

"You need to talk to the high priest group leader so you can be on the bus for the caravan from the stake," he told me.

So that's what I did. I went to the high priest group leader, raring to get to the temple . . . and hit a wall.

"There's no more room," he said.

Unbelievable. I was ticked. I had waited so long, worked so hard, given up so much, and now there was no room. But I wasn't going to be denied. I had just collected a lot of money for the doctor and, at that moment, saw him walking down the hall.

"Can you give me a check tomorrow?" I asked, a plan already forming in my mind. "Yes," he replied.

Some months earlier, after I'd joined the Church, I told my sister about my decision, thinking she was in for a surprise. But I was in for an even bigger one as she told me about her son. "Gary's a bishop in your church."

"He is?" I said, stunned. I didn't even know he was a member. Turns out he was a bishop in Sandy, Utah, at the time. So I called him up shortly after finding out there was no room for me on the bus to the temple. We talked all about the Church, my conversion and his, and how ours lives had taken such dramatic turns.

Then came my proposal, my plan.

"I want to fly out to Salt Lake and go through the temple with you," I told him.

"Yes, absolutely," he said, inviting me to stay the weekend.

I got a real good deal on the ticket and, since the doctor was going on the temple trip, I could be gone for a few days.

Why I called my nephew, to this day, I don't know. He was all excited that I was a member, his uncle joining the church. I don't think he could really believe it. I was on the plane, on the way out, when I remembered that one of the elders who'd baptized me was from American Fork. I decided I was going to give him a call. I got to my nephew's house, met his wife, and we talked for a while about everything. Then I borrowed his phone to call Elder Dwight Staples.

"I'm here in Salt Lake City and I'm going to the temple," I told him. He said he wanted to go through with me.

"I've got a surprise for you," he said. "When we get out of

the temple, I'll show you."

So my nephew and I met up with him at the Jordan River Temple. The three of us participated in a session together. It really was an amazing experience, even more than I'd thought it'd be. My nephew was great. He really helped me a lot that first time, helping me understand a little better what was going on. We did another session and when we were through, I was just overwhelmed. We sat in the Celestial room until the workers told us we had to leave, that they were closing for the day.

As we left the temple, Elder Staples pulled out his missionary journal. As promised, he had something to show me. He opened it up to where he'd written about the third discussion with me back in Detroit. It was the discussion when I had first seen the movie of the Washington, D.C. temple.

He'd written, way back then, that he knew he'd go through with me when I went to the temple for the first time. He wrote that, knowing he lived in American Fork and I lived halfway across the country. Never mind that I hadn't even joined the Church at that point. I was stunned.

"You wrote that after the third session with him?" my nephew asked him incredulously. He was really amazed by what he read.

"Yeah," Elder Staples answered. "And after I wrote that, I looked at it and read it and thought, 'How can this ever be? The man lives in Michigan and I live in American Fork and there isn't any way that I could afford to go back there and he doesn't have any relatives out in Utah.'"

Well, I didn't know that my nephew was a police chief out in Midvale and bishop out in Sandy at that time. I had lost track of that part of the family. I hadn't seen my nephew in twenty years. My sister had just packed up and left without a word to any of us. It was just mind-boggling how it all came about. It was another irony too amazing to explain away by coincidence. A higher power was definitely at work. And that power, the same that sent my troubling dream all that time ago, had also been at work on those missionaries though I didn't get the full story until that day with Elder Staples.

Apparently, the day the missionaries ended up on my doorstep and got that phone number from Lynette, they had actually been on their way somewhere else. Elder Staples, he'd been out a while and was a zone leader. His companion, Elder Gardner, was new. They were driving down Nine Mile Road that day when Elder Gardner pointed out my street.

"Wow, have you ever been down that road?" he asked Elder Staples. "It looks interesting."

Elder Staples looked down the road. "Yeah, let's go down there."

He made a U-turn, something he never should have done, and headed back. It was a dirt road with homes on two- to three-acre lots, kind of a rural setting in the middle of suburban Detroit. They drove down the street, past about twenty-five houses, and pulled into my driveway. Another rule broken. Missionaries don't park in the driveway, they leave the car at the curb in front of the house.

They walked up to the door as Elder Gardner pulled out specific pamphlets he wanted to leave. Lynette should not have been there to answer the door, usually she was at work. So many things had come together to bring me to the Church, I saw that now. Elder Staples's journal entries and memories of how he ended up at my front door only confirmed what I'd known for a while. There was a purpose for me.

That first Sunday I was back in Michigan, the bishop came up to me and asked, "How come you didn't come with us to the temple? The high priest group leader said there was plenty of room."

"You've got to be kidding me," I said.

Later, I asked the high priest group leader about it and he said he'd never told me the bus was full.

"But I remember you telling me there was no room," I insisted.

But it was no use. There had been room, but just not for me, I guess. The trip out west was meant to be. I know the Lord wanted that to happen and Elder Staples also had the faith, so it happened.

It wasn't two weeks after getting back to Michigan that I made a trip to the Washington, D.C. temple. I went with a couple of other guys and did the red-eye special. We'd leave Friday night, drive all night, work in the temple all day, drive back all night.

I did that twice a month for almost a year. In that time, I did fifty-five sessions.

E I G H T E E N

I belonged.

I'd only been a member for about five months when the bishop called me in his office one Sunday.

I was battling the fallout of my decision to leave the business. I had no education. I was getting eaten up by the lawyers, and my wife was divorcing me.

So, with all that going on in my life, the bishop says to me, "Next Sunday, I'm going to set you apart and give you a calling to be the Blazer A teacher and I also want you to get involved in the Scouting program."

When I was little, we used to beat up Boy Scouts, chase them through the streets, and here I was going to be a Boy Scout leader?

And there was the little problem that I had with not being too good with reading.

"Teach a class?" I replied weakly. "I can't even read and you want me to teach. What are you, crazy? I can't do that."

"You're going to do it," he said, standing up in front of me. "Are you turning your back on the Lord? Don't you think the Lord is going to help you?" That was like giving me a sock in the kisser.

All week long, I was a basket case. He gave me the manual and I talked to the old teacher. I tried to pretend like I knew what I was going to do. I didn't have anyone to go to for help. I just couldn't go up to another member and say, "I don't know how to read" and have them them say, "You jerk. Why did the bishop call *you* to that calling?"

So that Sunday, I walked into the church ready to tell the bishop that there was no way I could do what he was asking. I was talking to another guy when the bishop came up and put his arm around me.

"Are you ready?" he asked.

"Yeah, yeah, yeah," I answered.

We walked to the room and he kept walking. I went inside and there were three kids sitting there, waiting . . . for me . . . their teacher.

I looked at them.

They looked at me.

"Hey, guys," I said. "I don't know what I'm doing. I'm completely lost here, so I'm really going to have to depend on you to help me out, because I'm so new."

We pulled out the table and we all sat around it as I pulled out the manual. I was as slow at reading as they were. But we got through one lesson. We read the scriptures and we learned together.

I taught for six months. What a growing experience it was. Those kids taught me so much. Just knowing that their parents had taught them up to that point to be so obedient, so true to the gospel, to have the knowledge they had, it was amazing.

They were teaching *me* things. After that first week, I actually looked forward to our meetings on Sundays. Even during the week, we'd communicate. I did a lot with Scouting. When we'd get together to do our Scouting thing, we'd sit down and shoot the breeze about the lesson. I'd bring the book and they would ask, "Well, what are we going to do *next* Sunday?"

So we would write down scriptures and they would go home and look them up and I'd look some up, too. Then we'd get together on Sundays and share what we'd learned. It was such a fun thing, I felt like a little kid. Everything I ever wanted to know about God, this earth and why we're here, these kids were telling me. I really learned an awful lot from those boys.

One kid really figured me out to a peg. When we were alone he'd say, "It's okay, Brother Facione. I'll help you out. I know you can't read. I won't say anything. When I learn things in school, I'll tell you." So we had this little agreement between us.

Those three boys and I had a deal. Once we were all frustrated trying to figure something out and we didn't want to ask anyone else because it would have been embarrassing.

"Ah, damn it," I said.

Silence.

They all looked at me.

"Oh, I'm sorry boys," I said, immediately sickened at what I'd said. "From now on, we'll never use the Lord's name in vain or any other swear words." I used to carry 3x5 cards on me, so I wrote a promise to the Lord that none of us would ever swear. I signed it and they signed it.

Anytime we wanted to swear, we'd look at our card and that would remind us. I still have mine. There's a lot of experiences that happened when I was new in the church that put the frosting on the cake for me, but teaching those boys, that that was the best frosting of all.

It was sweet.

N I N E T E E N

Ma was in her familiar place, in front of the stove, frying pan in hand, as she made an omelet-like dish we all loved. She had that pan in her grip, moving it around as the omelet slid side to side, cooking until it looked almost like pie. We used to love to watch her make it.

So there I was, over at my folks' house, watching that omelet slide when I decided to break the news.

"Ma. I joined The Church of Jesus Christ of Latter-day Saints," I said.

"What?" she said, stopping in her tracks.

I repeated what I'd said and the next thing I knew the frying pan was sailing through the air towards me. The omelet was flying all over and the pan hit the wall, handle first, where it stayed.

I ran to the bathroom and hopped out the bathroom window to escape. She really wanted to get at me. She was very mad.

She wouldn't have nothing to do with me for a couple years after that. She thought I was going to be a disgrace to the family. It wasn't until years later, when she learned my nephew was a member, that she accepted it. She realized that if that's what I wanted to do, that was fine. My dad, he didn't care one way or another about my joining.

Neither did my Uncle John. He was a great old guy who'd been like a second father to us kids. He was always working on his trucks when we were growing up and he never married. My dad worked hard but when you have eight kids, it all went fast. So Uncle John was like a dad to us. He was the kind of guy that always made you realize that you had to do things right.

By 1983 I had gotten a job as a manufacturer's representative and I was traveling quite a bit selling industrial tooling. That line of work fit right in with me, having worked with trucks and all that. I was traveling around the country, visiting customers and attending shows where we'd set up with our tools and have people go through and see what we had.

I was out on a business trip when I got a call from my sister that Uncle John was very ill. I came right home and went to the hospital. He was already on life support.

The doctor said his insides were full of cancer. He was ninety-one years old. I was really close to my uncle and I could barely stand to see him connected to all those machines. I didn't want him to go on like that. The doctors said he wouldn't last long, that he was suffering. They advised taking him off life support.

My brothers and I, we were his legal guardians so the decision was ours. That's the way he had it set up. And I was the one who had to sign. So I did. I herded the doctors out and I signed.

But I wanted to give my uncle a blessing before they actually turned off the machines. The doctor was going to do that after we all left the room and then tell us when he passed away. I asked the doctor, could I give him a blessing?

It was amazing because there was this doctor, nurses and my brothers in the room; but when the doctor left, they all left.

The room was empty. So I gave my uncle a blessing.

"Lord," I prayed. "Please give me a little time with him. Just enough time to teach him a little about the gospel before he leaves the earth."

I prayed with all I had in me. I was drained. Every bit of energy was sapped out of me while I was giving that blessing. When I stopped, I turned and looked at the door and felt this great comfort. I turned back toward my uncle briefly before going out to see my brothers.

"I'll be back tomorrow." I told them as I went to leave.

They followed me down the hall, furious.

"The doctors have told us that Uncle John will die ten or fifteen minutes after they pull the plug," one said. "So where are you going?"

They couldn't believe I was leaving. But I did. I just went home and poured my heart out to the Lord. I just wanted that time with Uncle John because I'd never taken the time before. The prophets had always said that we should work with our families, try to share the gospel with them. Well, I didn't do that and here was Uncle John, at death's door, and he didn't know. I just knew he shouldn't go back to heaven without knowing about the Church. He had lived an illiterate life; the only thing he could do was sign his name.

That night, I prayed and prayed until I felt there were no more prayers in me. I went to bed. No call from the hospital. Got up the next morning and jumped in the shower; still no call.

I was back at the hospital by 8 A.M. and they had moved him to his own room. No one could believe he was still alive. I walked in that room and he held out his arms to me. He couldn't talk because he had a tube down his throat. I gave him a big hug and a big kiss.

My brother looked at me and just shook his head.

"How did you know this would happen?" he asked me. "By all rights, he's supposed to be gone. The doctors can't believe he's alive."

I just sat there talking to my uncle and he understood everything I said to him. The nurses were totally amazed. I took them aside.

"I'll be here every morning at 8 A.M. and I'll stay until 2 P.M. so you can do what you need to do," I told one.

I couldn't believe how they accommodated me. Every morning when I arrived, they had him bathed and fed. When Uncle John saw me, his eyes were bright.

"If you can hear me, raise your hand," I'd tell him. Up his hand would come. He was hard of hearing but he heard what I was telling him.

We started to talk.

I told him about the Plan of Salvation, how Jesus Christ had died so we might all live again after our death here on earth. I talked to him about things in the scriptures, about the teachings of prophets, ancient and modern.

This went on for almost two weeks. I'd talk to him all day and go home to my apartment at night. I'd dive into the scriptures, getting stuff ready for the next day. I'd go back with my folder as the nurse would go out the door.

Not a soul would come in there. My family would often come in after 2 P.M. Sometimes I'd stay, but often Uncle John would go right to sleep. The next morning he'd be wide awake, waiting for me to come.

On that final day, I sat on the edge of his bed, looking into his eyes.

"When the time comes, you'll be ready and I'll do the work for you," I said. He raised his arms to me and I gave him a hug. I walked out and left.

I knew he'd accepted what we'd talked about. He died that night at 11 P.M., almost two weeks after he'd been taken off life support.

A year later, I went to the Washington, D.C. temple, intent on doing his baptismal work. There was a group of youth waiting to do baptisms and my eyes stuck on one boy, my eyes just glued to the back of his head.

I went up and put my arm around him and asked him his name. He told me and I responded, "How would you like to do a baptism for my uncle?" He said yes. I approached his leaders and asked if he could do one special name for me and they went ahead and did it. He was baptized for my Uncle John. After the baptism, I did the confirmation and gave him the Holy Ghost. Then I went ahead and did the rest of his temple work.

I was sitting in the endowment room, at the end of a bench, thinking about the past. Uncle John had always meant so much to me, I thought, and this was one way I could repay him, by doing his work in the temple.

I turned and there he was, sitting on the bench next to me. I felt like there was an arm around my shoulder, I felt a squeeze. To this day I swear he was sitting there next to me. But when I turned back and looked, there was no one there. Just then, others starting coming into the room to prepare for the next session, filling the rows in front of and behind me.

All around me, people sat, except in the place right next to me. Uncle John's place.

There have been many times when I've had a dream or I'm driving down the road and things come to mind about him and the things we talked about when I was a kid, the things we talked about those final days of his life.

He accepted it, the whole nine yards. I'm sure of it.

TWENTY

The man sat there in the chair before us, a group of men weighing his fate. He'd done wrong, he knew it and it was up to us to decide what would happen to him.

On the surface, it could have been a scene from my past, but it wasn't. This time, the man in the chair had violated a commandment of the Lord and we, the high councilmen, had gathered to listen to his confession and pray for inspiration on how best to handle the situation.

"I've got to ask you a question," I said to the man seated before us. "How much have you been studying the scriptures in the past month?"

"Not much," he replied. "I really haven't had the time."

"Wait a minute, wait a minute," the words shot out of my mouth. "Don't hand me that stuff, that you don't have time.

You had time to go out and fool around. You're going to sit here and tell me now that you didn't have the time to read the scriptures?"

"These guys over here might pussyfoot around with you, but you're not pussyfooting around with me," I continued. "If you would have been keeping your face in the Book of Mormon like the prophet told you to do, you wouldn't be in this mess you're in today."

He looked back at me, the tears starting to flow down his face. He got no sympathy from me.

"Hey, what's crying going to do for you?" I said. "The truth hurts. I'm telling you like it is. I'm not saying you can't repent but the thing you've got to understand is that there's rules that you've got to go by. The *Lord* has set those rules down and what do you think the prophet is here for? He's here just to say he's an ornament? To say he's a prophet?

"The guy says read the Book of Mormon and why do you think he's been telling you that?" I kept going, firing away. "Because the morality part of the latter-days is the part that's dragging everybody down."

It tore me up to sit in on that Church court. I'd only been on the high council, a leadership body within the stake, two weeks and there I was, hearing how this guy had messed up. I put myself in the place of the Lord and after this guy was so blessed, having so many great things, he went and screwed up. What would that do to you? That would be devastating, I thought. I got mad and that's when I let loose my little tirade.

Afterward, the stake president took me aside and said, "Maybe next time you could go a little easier."

But I didn't know if I could.

Everything still comes down to a deal in my life, only this time the deal is between me and the Lord. Everyone who's been baptized in this Church has made the same deal. We agree to live by the commandments and the Lord gives us great blessings. He's made it even easier for us to know what to do by giving us a prophet to tell us and guide us. And what do we do? Head to the park or a vacation when General Conference comes around.

"Let's go, pack it up," so many members say each April and October when the prophet and other church leaders address the worldwide congregation of more than ten million. What they're really saying is, "Hey Lord, I really don't care to hear what you have to say today."

Who's not keeping up their end of the deal? So many do the same thing, think they can skate by and it'll work out in the end.

But it's not true . . . it's just not true. Just like with everything else, living the gospel is work. You got to work on it every day with all you have.

More than twenty-one years have passed since that night in the hotel room in Provo, the night of my dream. I often flash back and think about that. It was like the Lord was saying "You've got to take this direction. You've got to change your course but I can't tell you in a spiritual way because there is no spirit with you." So He tried to get the message to me in a way I might be able to understand, not having an education and all the other stuff that was going on.

And I didn't forget that dream. I'll never forget that dream.

The full meaning of the dream hit me like a ton of bricks on the day I was married and sealed in the Jordan River Temple to Cathy, a divorced member of the Church with three children, all of whom would be sealed to us. We'd be an eternal family, just like the ones I'd seen in that video all those years ago . . . a lifetime ago.

Our children—Amy, Scott and Jeff—all dressed in white, came into the sealing room. Now I really knew why the Lord had sent me the dream, the missionaries, and deliverance. The Lord needed me to help raise those kids. That was part of his plan. These kids are special, special people and, not that I'm any kind of superhero, but they needed the guidance. I knew right then and there that that was what it was all about.

I made a deal. There's no way of going back on it. I don't really know how to read. All I've got is street smarts and the knowledge of the gospel. But that special day in the temple just gave me all the more drive to go out and make it work.

Over the years, we've led a comfortable life; made a comfortable living though it will never approach the lifestyle I had before. I wouldn't want that anyway. But then, I never was overly concerned about the money. You cannot let it possess you. Once you let money possess you and control you, you're a loser. For me, it's always been about the challenge of making something work or seeing a plan succeed.

It's the same now only the deals are all legit and the money is earned. You strive to make something happen and work hard enough, it'll happen. You've got to work, to look for the next challenge. It's the challenge that continues to be the jet in my life.

I still hear something of the guys once in a while. After the initial hit on my money, they left me alone like they said they would. The heavy equipment scam ran its course not long after I left. Someone wised up and started putting identification numbers on the stuff, starting paying attention to where things went and how long they were gone. It wouldn't have lasted much longer, even if I had stayed.

Some of those boys are dead now, others ended up in prison. The feds went after them in a big way in the 1990s. The trials were front-page news in Detroit for months. The glory days are long gone for them.

Now, I work twice as hard as I've ever worked in my life because it's clean and I love every minute of it. But I'd never be able to do what I've done, any of it, if it wasn't for the Lord.

You set your sights in the way the Lord wants you to do it, not the way you want to do it, and it works out. Do it the way the Lord has set for you and you'll succeed every time. That's why the prophets tell us to set goals, to get an education, to always strive to be better.

It's funny that people don't always see it that way. Instead they look at a guy with money and think, "Oh, look at him. He's got all that money. That's not fair." They don't want to see that he worked for it, set a goal and went out there and earned it. You don't just sit there wishing, hoping it'll come to you. It doesn't.

It's the same with the gospel. "Why is he getting all the blessing?" some members wonder. "I read the Book of Mormon. I pay my tithing. Gee whiz, where are *my* blessings?"

My answer to that is, "Hey pal, what else are you doing?" Living the gospel is so much more than just doing the things on a list somewhere, it's a way of life, it's trying to make a difference in someone else's life.

The prophets haven't come right out and said it, but when you've got an idle mind, the hands get itchy. Things start happening that shouldn't be happening. The feet want to go places they don't belong. The mind starts wandering and then you start doing things that are totally against the principles of the gospel and the things the Lord wants you to do.

I did it wrong for a lot of years of my life. My dad showed me how to do things, but I took what he said and I used the information the wrong way. But by turning those ideas around and having that same drive and the same knowledge and applying it to gospel principles, you can accomplish great things.

If you let the gospel take its course and you grab as much as you can grab and the Lord releases to your mind what you're ready to accept, you'll conquer. You'll conquer, you'll absorb, and you'll always grow.

You do it because you want to win the deal. You want to end up on the other side and you want to be on the right-hand side of the Lord. That's my goal. My goal is to go and talk to Abinadi, go talk to all those guys. That's my goal, my dream. I want to talk to Joseph Smith. I want to talk to Isaiah. These people, they intrigue me. I want to see them so I've got to do what's right here on earth so I can. And I want to see my Uncle John, my parents, all who I loved who've died. And I hope when

I see them, they've accepted the gospel, that they've come to see in death what I was so lucky to find in life. I know they're waiting for me.

It all comes down to that ultimate deal and how much you want to be on the winning end. How bad do you want the gospel and how bad do you want to be on the right-hand side of the Lord?

My brother died a few years back and I was pretty tore up at first. We were pretty close and it hurt when he died. I used to call him up and we'd talk and he'd give me a lot of good ideas about things. I missed that and I miss him.

I grieved for about four hours and then I went into another room and prayed to the Lord to take care of him and give him what he needs, that hopefully he'd accept the gospel when I gave him that opportunity through temple work. I stood up and walked into the room where the rest of the family was gathered.

"That's it. Enough crying," I said. "I know what's going on on the other side so let's get down to business."

I oversaw the funeral arrangements and everything was taken care of. Some in my family said, "Boy, are you cold. What's the matter with you?"

"What? It's done with. It's over," I replied. "I know what's going to happen now."

They looked at me and one said, "What do you mean you know?" I didn't explain beyond saying, "Look, everything will be fine and someday you'll understand."

I walked away from it. I knew where he was. I know the plan. Thank God, I *do* know the plan.

If I die tomorrow, I've fulfilled my mission. I know in my heart that everything I've done since I've joined this church will leave something to better the lives of these people. Other than that, it was all meant to be.

I wouldn't do anything different in any way, shape or form.

ABOUT THE AUTHOR

Mario Facione is a successful businessman who lives in Michigan with his wife. They have three grown children and four grandchildren.